Psychic Development:

A Practical Guide to Developing Your Psychic Abilities

~ A Friend to Friend Series ~

Mary Shannon

SCM
Publishing

Also by Mary Shannon

Chakras and Auras (2018)
The Only Tarot Book You'll Ever Need (2019)
Dream Interpretation (2019)
The Witch's Book of Love (2020)

First publishing in the United States by SCM Publishing

SCM
Publishing

Table of Contents

Introduction

Everyone is psychic. Yep, you heard me correctly - everyone, even your mother, is psychic. So why is it that we see being psychic as some unique skill for only certain people? Perhaps because we, as a society, have chosen to squash our natural abilities and retrain our focus away from what we are born with.

In our modern society it is more important for our everyday survival to know how to find an answer in a book or on the computer rather than knowing how to ask our inner self and spirit guides. We may even gloss over that gut instinct that tells us what we should do, preferring the advice of someone we see as a wise friend or colleague. This has left us great at everyday life tasks but sometimes flailing around trying to figure out what our passions are or what our purpose in life really is.

We have the ability to regain and retrain these skills so that our natural intuitive abilities are alive and well - to figure out how to combine the importance of book learning with trusting our intuition and awareness. And yes, we can also start to understand other people on a deeper level as well.

What we first need to do is demystify what it actually means to be psychic. A psychic isn't necessarily what you see being portrayed in movies or on the tv screen. Psychic abilities are more subtle and take time and energy to perceive. This means you aren't necessarily going to see the ghost of your great aunt Myrtle cooking Sunday dinner when you visit your parents' house, but you may smell a whiff of her perfume or see the image of her favorite apron in your mind's eye.

Don't get me wrong though, there are some (a very few) people who will perceive her actual spectral figure, it just isn't exactly likely that this is going to be you after reading just one book unless you have some really great natural abilities. Even the psychics and mediums with their own tv shows don't see the actual physical ghost but instead receive images and words in their mind - this is how psychic ability works.

The thing about psychic abilities and honing your own natural skills, is that you have likely been experiencing these phenomena throughout your life, but your mind has been too busy focusing on the tangible world that you bypass or just ignore the information you are receiving.

Throughout this book we are gin to work on recognizing your own innate psychic abilities and then we will work on strengthening them and enhancing them. Like any of those muscles in your body, the more you use and pay attention to your psychic abilities the easier and stronger that skill is going to become.

After exploring the different types of psychic information you may receive and what they look like, we will walk step by step through the process of how to actually retrieve that information from your intuitive senses, starting with a little work on protective practices to help keep your energy shielded and your confidence up.

Then I will give you some exercises to work on to really build your intuitive muscle. What makes this book a little different from most other psychic development books on the market is that I focus on exercises that can be done independently, without a partner. Most can even be done in just a few minutes a day, so you will not need to develop hours every day developing your psychic abilities or find a like-minded individual who is working on using their psychic senses as well. This can be an independent activity if you like and I will give you a variety of exercise you can choose from to use.

After going over some general tips and information about the psychic world, we spend a little time on the ethics of psychic readings. I am not going to tell you what you should or should not do in terms of your abilities, instead I will give you some situations and questions to think about to help you develop your own internal ethics. Ethical systems work best if you believe in them and creating your own is the best way to do this.

By the end of this book I hope that you realize that you have been receiving psychic insight your entire life but now you understand how to perceive it and control it to better your life. I am here to give you the tools to help you understand your own abilities, it is up to you to use them and develop into the intuitive being that you are. You have been psychic all your life, now it is time for you to understand this skill which has always been available to you.

Psychic Basics

How do you feel when you hear or read the word psychic? Does it make you feel all warm and cozy or do you feel some ickiness and shame surrounding the word? Before we really get into developing your skills, we need to have an open and honest conversation about this word we are tossing around.

For a long time now, our culture has represented psychics in a negative light. People seem to shy away from calling themselves psychic or even using that term – I know I did (and sometimes still do). Instead you will see people use the term "intuitive" as a replacement for the term psychic. I have even seen better known figures in the metaphysical field offering classes to enhance your intuition – not psychic development classes. I have used the term intuitive to describe myself on social media – an intuitive clairvoyant.

But am I really an intuitive?

This question was on my mind when I encountered the word intuitive and intuition in the non-woo woo setting. I started watching a Netflix movie about intuition and it became quickly clear that what they called intuition and what I do are two very different things. I even read an article on a friend's Facebook post about how intuition is a sign of genius even quoting Albert Einstein's phrase "the only real valuable thing is intuition".

Although I think of myself as pretty intelligent, it became clear to me quickly that the genius level thinking that this article talks about has nothing to do with what I do during intuitive readings. Simply put, I am not using my intuition during these readings, I am using my psychic skills.

So how do I define intuition? My favorite analogy to use on the subject actually comes from an astrology book of all places – Bernadette Brady's <u>Predictive Astrology: The Eagle and the Lark</u>. She starts off the book with a little fable about larks and eagles, but I can't really remember all the details right now and I don't want to go rummaging through my too large collection of astrology books to find it, and really, it isn't very important. The point she makes is that with predictive astrology, you have to learn the basics and use them repeatedly and for a long time, and then, once you get really good at them, you will be able to spot patterns without really thinking about them and you will "intuitively" know which parts of a person's chart are important. She uses intuition the same way the Netflix movie uses it. Intuition as highly advanced pattern recognition in which your unconscious is able to spot patterns without you consciously thinking about them. That is intuition.

Now what do I do when I preform an "intuitive reading"? I do not believe I am spotting patterns. All I have is an individual's name and sometimes birthdate and I'm telling them the different colors of their aura and describing pictures of long-deceased relatives. I am seeing images in my third eye and faintly hearing words and songs inside my head, getting gut reactions and knowing facts out of seemingly nowhere. This is not intuition – this is not pattern recognition – this is clearly psychic work. So why do I not always call myself a psychic all the time? Why do I keep using the term intuitive to describe the work I do even though it is clearly not high-level unconscious pattern recognition?

Well, a lot of that centers around the energetics of the word "psychic" and what we have allowed people to put onto it. When individuals do not understand something, when it doesn't fit their framework of reality, sometimes they condom it. And psychic abilities do not fit in with the framework we are taught and the culture many of us live in. The word psychic is associated with frauds and back parlor tricks not spiritual connections and messages from the other side.

I believe we all need to work on becoming more accepting of the term psychic and reclaim it from the negative cultural connotations that it is associated with. We need to stand up and say I am not an intuitive clairvoyant but a psychic. Accept yourself as a true psychic - accept that you are developing your psychic abilities not your intuition.

It is okay to use both terms and to pay attention to which term to use when, but don't let yourself be fooled over the term. This is a book about learning to connect and decipher energy not a class in pattern recognition.

Psychic Ability or Imagination

In this book we are going to establish that you have psychic abilities, even if you don't realize it, and that they aren't what the movie industry or society has told you they look like - you aren't going to see a physical spectral of Elvis walking through your living room and you aren't likely to suddenly know the winning lottery numbers. Instead, psychic insight is much more subtle - flashes of images in your mind's eye, a word or two in your head, an icky feeling in the pit of your stomach, that information you just know.

One thing that is important to distinguish early on in your psychic development is when you are actually receiving and picking up on energy and information and when it is just your imagination gone wild. Imagination plays a strong part in helping to strengthen your abilities and they look very similar to actual psychic skills, so it is easy to get the two confused. You may have even told yourself for years that those little psychic experiences and intuition you have had are just your overactive imagination.

But, with a little practice and discernment, you will soon find it easy to pick up when you are actually just imagining your grandmother's favorite perfume and when it is actually a psychic indicator. You will be able to have outside confirmation and assure yourself that you are not making up what you are experiencing but it is actually there and true.

So, how do you do this? How do you distinguish between your imagination and psychic input? For this I am going to give you an exercise that involves clairvoyance, or "clear seeing", as an example to help you distinguish the two. Clairvoyance is the most common type of psychic ability that is talked about, but in the next section I'll walk you through all the other types of psychic abilities as well so don't worry about the difference yet.

When you get a clairvoyant image in your mind's eye, you are seeing a picture. For an example of this skill, I want you to picture a pink bunny rabbit wearing a purple tutu. That image right there is where you will see your psychic images and generally what your clairvoyant images will look and feel like.

With psychic readings, it is going to be important to realize and distinguish when that thing you see in your mind's eye is really a "hit" on the psychic train and when it is merely your imagination playing games with you. You can just as easily create this bunny wearing a tutu in your mind's eye as you can receive that information as psychic energy.

To distinguish the difference, it is helpful for beginners to use a psychic tool. Here I am not talking about tarot cards or runes (we will discuss those more later), I am talking about a psychic tool in your mind. Some people use a screen. They imagine a giant projector or movie screen in their mind's eye and see what images are portrayed on it. Anything to the side or not on a screen they know is not psychic information.

What I liked to do in my early day of psychic development is use an "opening" like a door or a window. I would get in my raised vibratory state (we will talk about this next), ask my question, and see what images appear when I open the door I created in front of me. This exercise is helpful because it uses both your imagination and your psychic abilities together.

Here is what you do. First picture a door in front of you in your mind's eye (that place where the bunny in the tutu resides). Imagine all the little details on the door. Where is the door handle? What color is the door? Is there any decorations on the door? What is the door made out of? Take the time to really create a door. You can use this same image again and again or change it each time. The door can be as elaborate or simple as you choose - a plain brown door works just as well as a glass door engraved with unicorns and butterflies.

After you have your door firmly placed in your mind, ask your question. We will talk about the phrasing of questions in a later chapter, but for now you can just use any question you want to know the answer to. A simple common question can be "What is my energy like today". Once you have asked the question, open the door and see what images appear.

If you feel your mind struggling to create an image in front of you like you did to create the door, then you know that this is just your imagination at work. But if the image appears suddenly and without any work on your part, then you can be sure it is a true clairvoyant image.

Another way to tell if an image or insight you are receiving is from the psychic realm or not is to pay attention to what you are currently experiencing. If you have been thinking about your dog all day and then see a mental image of a dog, it may just be that your imagination is thinking about dogs. But, if you "see" an image of a marching band and you have not been to a parade recently or have any connections with marching bands – it may just be that a marching band is your psychic symbol for something.

This trick also works with clairaudience (clear hearing) too. A lot of the time it is difficult to discern whether it is just your voice in your head talking, or if it is your guides or higher self getting information through.

With the words, you hear or the songs that just randomly pop into your head, pay attention if there is any reason for you to hear or think about those words recently. If you just heard Jingle Bells on the radio and then you hear it playing in your head, that likely is just you, not your super awesome psychic abilities sending you a message. But if you hear Jingle Bells in the middle of August and haven't thought about that song

since last December – then, yes, that is probably a psychic
message coming through.

I have found that it is very useful to practice this discernment
every day. It is only through practice that you are going to
learn what images, sounds, or information "feel" like in your
imagination or mental chatter and which ones are truly
psychic insights. This is one reason I "read" the energy of
myself every morning – tapping into the energy grid and
"seeing" what I see. It is through doing this exercise that I
learn what is just me and what is something else.

Raising Vibrations: Getting into the Psychic Zone

Now you know how to tell the difference between something
that is actual psychic information and something that is just
your imagination (or at least you are on your way), let's discuss
how to actually get into the psychic zone where information
comes easier and clearer.

One reason there may not be anything behind that door you
created in your mind is because you are not in the right
vibratory state to receive information. Yep, we are talking
about the new age idea of raising your vibes. Yes, this is a real
thing and not something just woo-woo people encounter.

Why is it important to raise your vibrations??

First, let's start off with the "why". Let's look at this from a
psychic standpoint. When tapping into the energy source that
has all this information, it is important for us to "raise our

vibrations" simply because the information is contained at a higher vibrational level.

When we raise our vibrations, it allows us to gather more information and live in a place where we have a greater connection to other dimensions. Now, what do I mean by other dimensions?? For some, this could mean it brings you closer to heaven, like a heaven on earth – experiencing the vibratory rate of heaven (or getting close to it) while still on earth.

But heaven is a loaded word, and it is just that, a word. We can also say "the other side" or "across the veil" or "that place we go when we die" or "akashic records". Whatever you want to call it, by raising our vibrations we get closer to that spiritual place. We are able to access the information and the entities that are located in that place at a greater frequency.

What does this mean? By raising your vibration, you can "talk to dead people". You can get into contact with your deceased loved one, your spirit guides, and even your higher self. You can also "read" the energy field (also a higher vibration) around people and thus tell them what their aura looks like or what they have experienced in the past.

There is a reason we don't see or experience these things in our daily life - or at least don't recognize them. What we call psychic information is just vibrations that exist on a different level. Just like we can't see infrared with our eyes, we can't pick up on psychic information with our common five senses. But we can raise our vibratory state to make it easier to pick up the information that exists at that state.

What does energy feel like??

You will find a lot of articles out in the inter-webs about
different ways to raise your vibration. Some people swear by
eating certain foods while others say you need to meditate
daily. But, really, you can learn to raise your vibrations by
moving energy up through your body and to a higher place.

But first, you have to learn how to move energy through your
body. This takes time, patience and actual effort – I know, I
am going to make you do some homework. Feeling and
moving energy is a skill that takes practice, but it is totally
doable. You can learn this from a variety of places and
methods, but it is available to everyone.

The sensations of moving energy are subtle. I like to start with
taking the energy that is in my body and pushing it into the
ground – aka grounding your energy. To do this, it may help
to stand up straight, with your feet hips distance apart. Close
your eyes and "feel" energy leaving your body and going into
the ground, growing out of you like the roots of a tree.

Next, take that energy and pull it from the roots of the tree
back up. Move this energy up through your legs and along
your spine, hitting each chakra center, until it finally moves out
the top of your head. But, don't stop there. Continue to move
this energy up into the air as high as you can get it to go.

Don't be surprised if you can't "feel" this energy the first time
you do it (or even the fifteenth). This is the type of exercise
that takes daily practice. But the more you do it, the easier it
will be and then one day, everything will just click, and you
will realize you have been feeling, moving, and directing this
thing called "energy" for weeks now.

What does it feel like to raise your vibration??

Everyone will feel differently when they have raised their vibrations. But, even so, I find it helpful to hear other people's experience, so I thought I would tell you guys a little about my experience with a raised vibration.

When I get into that raised vibratory state, I know I am there by that tone and pitch of the ringing in my ears. Yes, certain types of ringing in the ears is bad and a medical condition, but sometimes when you hear a ringing it is a sign that you are "listening" to a higher vibratory rate. When I get to this place, I can "hear" my guides and other people's guides better. And there are different levels of this. This "higher" I go, the higher and stronger the pitch gets.

When I have a raised vibration, I am better able to see the energy around me. I can literally see (not just in my third eye) the energy around me as static, like on a tv screen. Energy can look different depending on where I am, but the most common occurrence when I get in this raised vibratory state is that static appearance.

Additionally, I will feel a calming down of my mind. This is a very peaceful and serene feeling that just forgets about any of the worries of the day. It also "feels" like I have a "knowing" that everything is going to be alright. I also generally feel a slight pressure or tingling sensation on the left side of my cheek, an indication that my main spirit guide is present and ready to assist.

Other activities to help

This idea of raising your vibration by moving energy is a great start for any beginner. It will help you get in the correct frame of mind even when your true vibratory rate isn't high all the time. There are other methods to get your vibratory rate higher throughout your daily life and it is in these states where you can then release the practice of "trying" to get in a higher energy state and just "be" in it at a moment's notice.

To raise your vibration every day you can look towards activities like meditation and paying attention to the food you eat. Certain food is lower vibration than other foods. You can also pay attention to the media you consume and what your general outlook on life is. Spending time learning about spirituality and taking on a spiritual outlook on life also helps raise your vibration.

Our general population and culture right now aren't at the vibratory rate that results in instant psychic access. There is a general shift that happens with individuals when they are able to see the world with a sense of unity and purpose instead of victimhood and crisis that needs to happen, and we just aren't there yet. But that doesn't mean you can't get there yourself.

Choosing to work on raising your vibrations on a daily level is not necessary for psychic development but it helps. Basically, just having a general overall positive and spiritual outlook on life not only helps in your daily living but also with receiving psychic information. We don't really have time in this book to go into details about specific ways and tools to do this, but you will generally find the tools if you are ready and willing to - just ask your psychic senses. This is one of those instances where the correct information will just pop up in front of you for you to follow. It isn't something that you can do in a day - it is an activity that generally takes years but is available to all.

The Psychic Senses

Any basic entry level psychic development class or book will teach you about the different "clairs" – your extrasensory perceptions that you use to help gather information from the energetic world that you then use for your psychic predictions or assessments. And this book is no different!

So, what exactly are we talking about here? Different people experience psychic awareness in different ways. These different ways have been classified into different "clairs". Most are based off traditional senses just using those ideas in a metaphysical context.

Everyone can utilize all their clairs, but some are more sensitive to certain abilities than other people. Learning which abilities are your strong suit tells you where you want to focus your energies and attention. Once you have some comfort in that area, you can work on learning to understand your other clairs. In any case, it is helpful to know what each clair looks like and feels like so you know if and when you are receiving information in that manner (you don't have to remember the actual name though, so don't worry, there is no test at the end).

Let's get started.

Most people have heard the term clairvoyant and know that to mean someone who "sees the future". But what about the other senses and how to gather information in alternative ways?

First, I am going to walk you through what each of the clairs means but do so in a fun and playful manner that will help you to get a better understanding of these senses, after that we will look into each of the senses in more detail. Yep, that is right, we are going to have a little fun!!!

I'd like to introduce you to the "Clair" sisters – a group of teenage sisters who all are named "Clair"!

First, let's start with **clairvoyance – clear seeing**. "Clair"voyance is the sister in the pack that dresses like it is Halloween every day and wears what you would consider a stereotypical psychic would wear. She likes to carry around her crystal ball and will occasionally get quiet, stare into the ball and makes some archaic pronouncement.

Just imagine this sister sitting at the kitchen table, eating her cereal, when all of a sudden, she closes her eyes, puts her fingers to her forehead and announces, "I see a red **X** over a microscope". She then proceeds to talk about all the different things this image could mean, only later to understand that she had a quiz in her chemistry class that day and she got every question wrong (she was too busy daydreaming – aka refining her clairvoyant skills – the day before to listen to the teacher when he said there was a quiz the next day).

Next, let's talk about **clairaudience – clear hearing**. "Clair"audience always has her headphones near her. If they aren't over her ears, they are hanging around her neck. And not the wimpy earbuds kind of headphones. No, "Clair" prefers to have her entire ear covered to drown out any outside noise. This "Clair" is always humming a tune, which totally annoys her sisters.

When sitting around the breakfast table in the morning, this sis will proclaim, "today is going to be bright and sunny!". When her sister's ask how she knows, she will tell them that she just heard the song lyric "On the Sunny Side of the Street" playing in her head – and then she will go on to sing the full version until her sisters throw muffins at her to get her to stop.

From here, we move on to **claircognizance – clear knowing**. "Clair"cognizance is the sister who is just a know it all. You know the one, the one that is always right, even if you hate to admit it. She is the protectionist of the group, wearing her pink cardigan buttoned up and her hair in a tight bun.

At the breakfast table, this "Clair" sits down amid an already heated gossip session about the couples at school and tells her sisters that Barbie and Ken have broken up. All the sisters roll their eyes and "Clair"audience says there is no way that happened because Barbie and Ken have sworn undying love to each other. But, each sister knows that when they get to school, Barbie and Ken will most likely have had a falling out, because, no matter how much they argue, "Clair"cognizance is always right. She just "knows" things - and yes, this is super annoying.

Next up is **clairsentience – clear feeling**. "Clair"sentience wears yoga clothes night and day. She is always moving her body in some way and excels at any school sport she chooses to join, although right now she is just the head of the yoga club and refuses to join the dance team even though its members have practically begged her.

While eating her bowl of organic fruit at the morning breakfast table, she looks over to "Clair"voyance and says "Ugh, you have that headache again!! What have I told you about drinking too many cups of coffee in the morning? You need to lay off that stuff and drink water purified by reverse osmosis". "Clair"voyance rolls her eyes at her sister but has to acknowledge she does have that headache again.

Now we have the often forgotten – **clairalience – clear smelling**. "Clair"alience sits back at the kitchen island, not really in the cool crowd with her other sisters at the kitchen table. But she doesn't mind sitting back here near the smells of the kitchen.

This sister loves flowers because of their beautiful smell. She even put together beautiful arrangements that decorate each room of the house. This sister (along with the help of her parents because she is underage) has already started an essential oil business and regularly recommends oils to her friends and family members. Today she is sporting peppermint in her oil diffusing bracelet because she actually listened to the teacher yesterday and knows there is going to be a quiz in Chemistry, so she wants to be focused and on her game.

Finally, we have **clairgustance – clear tasting**. "Clair"gustance sits back at the breakfast bar with her sis "Clair"alience. They just aren't part of the "cool" sisters, but she is okay with that. She likes being near food. She likes the taste and all the ingredients.

While the other sisters are munching on their breakfasts, this sister takes the time and effort to cook up a veggie-tofu scramble and adds fresh organic fruit to the side of her plate. She is one of those "super tasters" and has strong opinions about what foods she is willing to eat. She has even become a vegan, much to the chagrin of her parents, because she swears, she can taste the suffering of the chickens in the eggs and the puss from the factory farming in the milk.

Finally, let me introduce you to the "Clair" sister's little brother, **Empath.** Em has some of the abilities of the other sisters, but he has the added ability to feel the emotions of others, especially when he gets too close. He isn't even sitting at the breakfast table, instead, he is up in his room just dreading going to school in the morning.

He hates school, in fact, he hates any activity that brings him in contact with a large number of people, but really, school is the worst. Rooms upon rooms filled with hormonal young people – the emotions just fly all over the place. By the end of the day Em likes nothing better than to head to swim practice where he can just do lap after lap and let the cool calming effects of the salt water (their school uses salt instead of chlorine – salt water is great for empaths) help to calm Em's nerves and bring him back to himself.

There you have it, the "Clair" sisters and their little bro "Em".

Clairvoyance

Okay, so now that you know the different types of ways you can sense psychic information, let's really discuss what receiving information in these different ways feels like. Remember, what Hollywood has taught you is not necessarily what people typically experience. Psychic abilities are a lot more subtle and hard to discern than what you imagined.

Clairvoyance is probably the most popular and talked about psychic ability out there. I say it is the most popular, but that is likely because it is the easiest to recognize. Who knows, the most popular psychic ability could be clairsentience, but people just don't recognize it easily, so they let it slip by.

Now, as we discussed previously, clairvoyance does not necessarily mean seeing your dead grandmother spooning out gravy in the kitchen in full detail and neither does it mean seeing detailed scenes of the future play out in front of you. It can and occasionally does look like this, but it is not super common to have this ability present in this manner. Instead, clairvoyance is typically much more subtle.

Just a side note here before we go farther. I keep using terms like "typically" and "usually" because I don't want to stereotype all abilities one way. Yes, there are a few people out there who actually can see ghosts in a clear manner, but those individuals are not likely reading this book because they don't need to be trained to use their clairvoyant ability.

So, let's continue, the thing about clairvoyance is that it utilizes your third eye, or that point between your eyebrows and up a little bit and then go back into your brain. Basically, your third-eye charka - but this isn't the book where I'm going to talk about chakras (I've got a different book for that if you are interested <u>Chakras and Auras: A Practical Guide to Your Energetic Body</u> - no harm in a little self-promotion here).

This is the location in your mind where you see images when reading a book or listening to an audiobook. This is where your mind paints pictures of majestic scenes from books or the details of the latest story your friend is reciting. This is where you have created and will continue to create pictures in your mind throughout your life.

Creativity and psychic ability are very much linked and using your imagination and mind to play out fantasias and possibilities helps train this center to receive psychic information. Yes, daydreaming is a great skill and exercise for this ability.

Now let's get down to it. We know that we receive psychic information as images in our mind's eye or third eye chakra, but what do the psychic images actually look like? Well, here is the thing. They are different depending on how you perceive information and how you train this ability.

Personally, I am a "symbolic psychic", I tend to receive information as symbols, or pictorial representations, that I then have to interpret to understand the meaning. This means that I may see the image of someone fishing and understand that as meaning "waiting". The image can then change to provide even greater context - the individual fishing could be an older individual or a young person - showing the characteristic of what part of my life I am waiting for something to happen - a new project or one that I have been working on for a while. The fishing could be taking place on a lake or in an ocean - speaking of the breath and scope of the waiting. The waves can be calm or fierce showing the emotions involved in this process. Any minor change to the scene then brings about a lot more information about what is happening.

That is the thing about symbols and why they are so widely used in psychic abilities, one symbol can convey a great deal of information in an instant whereas words would take a lot more time to provide. I can quickly glimpse the image of an old man fishing at sunset on a calm lake and understand the nuanced nature of that message. Whereas using words to describe the idea of waiting for a project to finish that has been going on a long time, but it will be a calm and relaxing ending - that takes a lot more time and effort to convey. The image of the man fishing can be glimpsed in a second.

Okay, so we now understand that information can be conveyed in symbols in your mind's eye or pictures which represent a message. But that isn't the only way information can be conveyed. Sometimes you will receive pictures in your mind's eye which are not symbols, instead you may receive information which is blatant and straightforward.

My favorite example of seeing actual images and the easiest for people to understand is some of the images I saw during my foray into mediumship. Mediumship is the ability to connect with individuals who are deceased. Many times, mediums will pick up symbols like in traditional psychic readings - they may say they see a cake which represents someone is celebrating a birthday. But other times information can be more direct. When I was training my mediumship abilities, I had instances of describing an exact sweater of an individual or the interior of a room. These images came in similar to my symbolic psychic images but would not have an easy translation from symbols. In these instances, I had the recipient of the message confirm what I was seeing as actual items.

In addition to either being symbolic or actual images, clairvoyant images are sometimes static and other times active. They may appear like a picture or a movie in your mind. You may even find that sometimes you have a strength in keeping a picture type image in focus but then may lose the image when it starts to "play" in a movie form.

You don't really need to worry too much about this right now. Instead, it is best to just let everything play out for you. The most important thing right now is to recognize what a clairvoyant image looks like and when you may be receiving them.

Clairaudience

Probably the second most prevalent psychic sense is clairaudience or clear hearing (again, I say probably here and not definitively). This is again one of those psychic senses which is dramatically exaggerated for Hollywood to a degree that people think you literally are hearing voices in your head - but that isn't quite what clairaudience really is.

I remember hearing a story that John Edward (the psychic, not the politician - yes, the one that had the show on tv - and yes, he is actually a good and legitimate psychic and medium) told about how he learned he was clairaudient. He started doing tarot readings when he was really young and at one point someone said (I think this was a fellow reader) that he was clairaudient. But he didn't think so because he wasn't hearing voices in his head. Instead, what this individual explained was that clairaudience is the same "voice" in your head that is you talking and thinking to yourself - not a literal voice that you hear with your ears.

This was a turning point for him in understanding what clairaudience really is and I believe it is something that should be taught right away to all developing psychics. You may be clairaudient and not even realize it because you are discounting that "voice" in your head that is talking to you and instead thinking that the information you receive needs to be heard with your physical ears to be clairaudient.

Nope. Just like with clairvoyance where you "see" in your "mind's eye", with clairaudience you "hear" that voice in your mind. Also similar is the difficulty that occurs when you are discerning what is just your mind making up pictures in your head, it can be difficult to sort out what is psychic information

coming from that voice in your head and just you talking to
yourself.

You can use similar methods to figure out if it is "just your
imagination" or true psychic insight as you do with
clairvoyance. Is it something out of the blue or something you
heard earlier in the day? Does the "voice" sound like
something you would say to yourself or is it advice you hadn't
thought of before?

The more you practice this distinction and pay attention to this
sense, the more it will develop and the easier it will be to figure
out when you are receiving information this way - but this is
how it is with everything isn't it - practice does help you
advance.

Something special with clairaudience is that, a lot of times, you
will receive songs that can be interpreted as symbolic messages.
These are the songs that just "pop" into your mind after not
hearing it for a long time. Usually some lyrics or emotions
associated with the song will provide a message for you. I've
even experienced times where I receive lyrics or song titles of
songs I have never heard of before. This is when internet
search engines come in handy to figure out what the message is
all about.

Music is important to a lot of people. I've written extensively
about the metaphysical power of music previously on my blog
as this is something that my guides have harped on over the
years. There are so many layers of vibration and power
available in music. I believe this is one reason why songs come
through so easily when people are working with their
clairvoyance. Music is a powerful medium and provides layers
and layers of potential energy to decipher.

Another thing you may notice with clairaudience is that the
more you practice, the longer statements and information you

will receive. At first, I could just get a word or two, may a sentence. But the more I developed and worked on this skill, the longer the statements and details of information would come through. Now I can receive paragraphs of information through clairaudience, but with this you have to learn to stay "in the zone" and "listening" and not get distracted - a difficult task for many people (yes, that means it is even hard for me sometimes).

Claircognizant

I am going to admit here that I actually expect Claircognizance to be the most prominent form of psychic ability, but it is also the hardest to quantify. Claircognizance speaks of having a "feeling" or "instinct" that tells you something. We have so many idioms in our culture that describe this psychic ability, but we don't give it the credit it deserves. How many times have to talked of "going with your gut" or "trusting your instincts" or a "mother's intuition"? This is claircognizance at its basics.

Many people may recognize this ability in themselves when they get that idea, seemingly out of nowhere, to go a different route to work only to later discover that there was an accident the way you traditionally would go. Or maybe you just know something is off with your neighbor down the street but you don't know why so you avoid his seemingly normal house, only later to discover he has been arrested for some insider trading (you didn't think I was going to go there huh).

One aspect of this ability that I have found very important to train it is your trust in the information you receive. Sometimes you don't know the "why" behind that idea to do or not do something. This is difficult for those wanting a rational reason to feel or think a certain way, but sometimes you need to throw that rational idea out the window. And sometimes you just need to trust that following that instinct was the right thing to do, even when you don't get confirmation that it was correct.

What I have found is usually you get confirmation on this ability when you don't follow it. You don't listen to that inner urge to go a different way to work and then you end up in a traffic jam for an hour. You befriend that neighbor down the street and find yourself involved in a scandal with your life savings held by the FBI. Yeah, you may want to follow this ability even if you don't know why.

The problem with going against this instinct and not trusting it just to see what happens is that you will eventually have a difficult time discerning it. The more you pay attention and trust this ability the stronger it will become. You will soon notice that you just "know" things and trust that you do not need to know the "why" behind those instincts.

Trust them and they will lead you down your chosen path.

Clairsentient

Clairsentience is an ability that easily gets mixed up with both claircognizance and empaths. In general, clairsentience is the ability to "feel" energy. This means feeling with your physical body. This is a skill that isn't really taught much and so is not always easy to understand.

The simplest way to think about this ability is if you hold an object in your hands and you notice that your hands "feel" a pulsing sensation or a vibration coming off the object. Many professional psychics do this technique, called psychometry, as an "anchor" to then use their other psychic senses to read more about an individual.

Clairsentience gets even more confusing when you realize that you can feel vibrations and energies throughout your body. Those with clairsentience may be able to pick up on certain areas of the body that hurt in another individual or when a colleague has a headache.

In contrast, empaths feel the feelings of other individuals as in emotions, not physical senses in the body. Sometimes, however, these feelings are associated with bodily sensations. For example, an empath may know that another individual is nervous because they feel a clenching sensation in the pit of their tummy associated with nervousness. A clairsentient may also know an individual is nervous in the same manner, but would also be able to distinguish if the person is nervous about a nail they stepped on earlier in the day because they will also feel a sharp pain on the bottom of their foot.

Clairsentience and empathy are similar but not the same. There is definitely some overlap there but still different enough to be distinguishable and part of the issue we have is one of definitions and words available to describe sensations. We are also working on labeling here when, instead, we could just categorize all these different senses into reading and experiencing energy without using any strict definitions and everything would still work out fine. Again, you do not need to label or even know the proper name for any of these abilities, but I do understand how it helps to understand them this way.

Also similar to empaths, individuals with clairsentience sometimes have a difficult time going into large crowds or working in office buildings with lots of individuals. This is because, if they do not know how to block vibrations out, they can end up picking up on the bodily issues of everyone in their vicinity. This can range from physical ailments to emotions since emotions are generally "felt" physically in the body.

Another easy way to tell if someone is clairsentient is through the idioms we use in society. Have you ever entered a room and felt that you could "cut the tension with a knife"? This is an example of someone sensing the energy and feeling the anger which is present. How about if someone feels "cold" to you, same thing.

Clairsentience is also one of those abilities where if you notice some of the characteristics in yourself you will want to pay attention on how to deflect the energy and how to shut yourself off so you don't end up reading everyone in a room. I'll give some techniques in the chapter on Psychic Protection so you will want to pay attention to those.

I find it very important to practice some of these protective techniques and they do work. In the past, I have had a difficult time going to movie theaters as I would physically shake from feeling too many of the sensations and energies from individuals in the theater. Just think of all the emotions that come up in individuals when they are watching a suspense film, now think of how many people would be experiencing the exact same emotions at the same time while in that theater. Overtime I understood and developed my ability to shield and protect my energy so I am now able to attend outings with more individuals present, although I do limit the settings I expose myself to. I find that situations where you are sitting or standing in one place and all experiencing the same emotions (i.e. movies or concerts) are more difficult than places where people are walking around and experiencing different emotions (hospitals or museums).

Clairalience

Clairalience is a less talked about psychic ability but one that many people may experience from time to time. This is the ability to pick up smells that are not present in the physical environment. Knowing whether or not you have this ability takes recognizing when a scent drifts in but a physical presence of that scent isn't anywhere in the vicinity which can sometimes be difficult depending the situation.

This is a way that I have heard many individuals experience visitations from a loved one who has transitioned. They will smell a particular perfume that they would wear or a flower that prominently bloomed in their garden. If you have mediumship abilities and want to deepen them to a greater level, it is important to actually know what some of these different smells or popular perfumes and cologne smell like so you can recognize them. I've watched mediums pick up Old Spice but, to me who does not recognize this fragrance, I would not be able to pass along this information.

Visitations are not the only time clairalience can be active. You may receive a certain smell to get your attention or provide information. A scent of rose could be a sign of love and affection you are picking up on or the scent of orange could mean cleansing to you.

I do not have a lot of experience with clairalience; however, I do have a distinct memory of smelling the scent of patchouli in a Barnes and Nobel once, not a location that would have that scent readily in the air. When I sensed this smell, I immediately stopped what I was doing and paid attention. With the environment I was in this meant looking at what books where right in front of me and, sure enough, a book I was interested in was right there on the shelf.

Clairalience may be a psychic ability that isn't given much attention, but it is one that can provide confirmation or knowledge that you would not have had otherwise. Don't discount this sense or its ability to be a useful tool.

Clairgustance

Now we get to the one psychic sense that I actually have never had any personal experience with, clairgustance. This is the acquiring of psychic knowledge through taste. Individuals who experience clairgustance may find they associate different tastes with certain people or situations.

Like clairalience, clairgustance's ability to inform depends on your sensitivity and knowledge of different tastes. For example, if you don't know what mango tastes like without a refresher of a bite, you may have trouble recognizing that this information is being sent.

The manner I have seen this ability most commonly used is when a psychic or medium has a metallic taste in their mouth which they associate with blood. This tends to mean that an individual had bleeding, perhaps though the mouth, at the time of a situation or their death.

One fun thing about clairgustance is that to develop it further it is important to taste a lot of different types of food. This can be a fun exercise and allows you to sample many delicacies. Just be sure not to rush the experience and let each taste bud recognize, savor and remember the flavors.

Empath

Many people have heard the term empath as it becomes more and more common to talk about in our modern culture. For a basic definition, an empath is someone who feels and picks up on the emotions of others. They act as emotional sponges picking up and absorbing the emotional states of those around them.

Empaths are different than the term empathy and this can cause some confusion. Empathy means to recognize and share the emotions of another individual. Empaths actually physically feel the emotions of other individuals in their own body, not just understanding another individual's emotions.

Empathy shares a lot in common with clairsentience as we have previously discussed because it is easier to understand emotions as feelings in your body. A nervous energy at the pit of your stomach or a tightness in your chest from anger. Whereas those with clairsentience who also feel these physical sensations and must learn to recognize and distinguish the emotions that are commonly associated with these physical sensations versus normal body sensations, empaths focus just on the emotional aspect of these bodily sensations.

To me, I kind of view empaths as clairsentience light, they have some of the same abilities of a clairsentient just not to the degree or specificity. Empaths have also started to become "trendy" in some new age or spirituality literature which leads many people to not only recognize this ability in themselves but to over-exaggerate it to a degree. Yes, everyone is empathic, but some are more so.

Those individuals that find they have a high degree of empathic abilities will have the same issues traversing environments with a lot of people just like those with clairsentience do. The same psychic protection techniques which shield those with clairsentience can and should be put into place for empaths who readily pick up on a lot of emotions.

How Psychic Information Appears

Now that we know about all the different ways you can receive psychic information, or detect different energy vibrations, let's take a moment to discuss what type of information you will receive.

This is something that I felt was missing in my early psychic education. I touched on this previously, but I wanted to expand a bit more here on this topic. When I was younger, I always thought I would receive straight forward information when doing psychic readings. I thought that when I was reading an individual who would ask about their future career, I would just see them being an accountant or a doctor in surgery. But this is not always the case.

Different psychics have different primary ways they sense information along with primary types of information they will receive. Yes, some psychics receive straight information about the subject they are reading, but others receive symbols.

I'm pretty passionate about talking about this subject as I feel that sometimes it is misleading of what psychic abilities actually are and this can be confusing and lead some people to not realize that they actually have abilities.

Being a symbolic psychic (I'm pretty sure I made up this term, but I like it!), early on in my development I would become easily discouraged reading accounts of other psychics that received more direct information. But then I started to realize that this was just how I function – and I'm not the only one out there that functions this way. In fact, many prominent psychics in the field operate off interpreting symbolic images, they just don't always tell you the image they receive, instead they just let you know their interpretation.

When I took my foray into mediumship I quickly realized that each spirit communicates differently. Some spirits are really good at communication and give detailed pictures of individuals, while others aren't as studied and are harder to interpret or understand what they are sending. I've also worked with a large number of spirit guides (spirit guides are like spiritual helpers guiding people on their journey through life), channeling information from them and have learned that each communicates in a different manner.

Through communicating with all these different spiritual entities, this also lead me to realize that my main spirit guide works chiefly through symbolism and symbolic images and this is why my main form of psychic insight comes from these highly symbolic scenes instead of blatant information. You can think of spirit guides as sort of your personal spiritual translator, helping communicate information from energy and spirit realms to you in an organized fashion.

There is a distinct reason many spirit guides prefer symbolism instead of direct information, which we discussed in the previous chapter, but as a reminder here - a symbol contains a lot more information than just words.

Imagine the scene of a ship out at sea with lighting and thunder. Already you can gain a lot of information from this image. Looking at the waves you can have the energy of feeling "battered" and "bombarded" by outside forces. The thunder and lightning can signal grumpiness and lashing out. The night sky can show a darkness and uncertainty to what is occurring. The state of the ship – whether it is whole or has been damaged – can show how someone is coping with this environment. The size and type of ship can show the general persona or state of the individual. See – so much information in one scene!

When you learn to put your abilities forward and read different situations or people, you will come to understand what type of information you primarily receive. It may be straight forward information, or it may be symbolic or some combination of both. There is nothing better or worse about either of these types of information.

If you decide to go down the mediumship route you will also learn that spirits communicate in different ways depending on their abilities. Some are strong and can communicate detailed information, others are more symbolic and still others have a difficult time relaying any type of information. Each encounter and experience is different and unique, just like people you interact with here on earth.

Building a Symbol library

One thing that some psychics say is helpful is to build up your own symbol library - a list of symbols you receive and what they mean to you. This is a way that you and your guides can work together to build a working vocabulary to use when you do readings.

Now, let me take a second and be really honest with you. I tried this method starting out. I had a book that I would write down all my symbols and their meanings…but after a while I just gave this up. It was too much to keep it going and it wasn't realistic with the amount of readings I do or the types of information I receive.

If you can remember your standard definitions of symbols, you may not need this. For example, I receive the image of a bouncing basketball from my guide as a symbol for an individual to go out and experience something new and different and then bring it back to their source. I don't feel like I need to write this down any longer because I just know and remember.

I have also found that sometimes guides will change up what the symbol means so having it be one solid definition is not really realistic. For example, tornados tend to mean destruction for me. But this can be nuanced. Sometimes in a reading a tornado may reference tearing down the foundations and structures that you have built. Other times a tornado may symbolize an outside force coming in and causing havoc in your life. For each circumstance I used my abilities to just "know" and "understand" which one my guide is pointing to.

So, while developing and using a symbolic library of your own may be helpful in the beginning, as you get more accustomed to your abilities and learn to understand symbols on a deeper level you may find that actually writing down your symbol library to be more cumbersome than it is worth.

And before I finish off this section, I want to just give a piece of advice about using symbolic dictionaries written by other individuals. These just don't work. You may have found that there are books out there of symbols and what they mean, but these are commonly universal meanings and not something to you personally. You will likely find that symbols you receive are much more personal in nature and not something that can be read in a book.

Symbols are also not always something that stay the same from psychic to psychic. Yes, to some psychics seeing a cake will mean a time of congratulations or celebration but it may also be a symbol to a different psychic to watch out for diabetes or that someone has a sweet tooth. Personally, I would bet that other psychics do not use the same definition I do with a basketball bouncing.

We tend to have symbols that come from our culture and personal experience. Depending on where we live, who we interact with, and what we experience in life, our symbols may change and evolve. This is why using a symbolic dictionary created by others is not always very helpful. They may live in a different country or culture and their ideas will not necessarily reflect your own. You can use these as a starting off point, or even just use the internet to search what things mean, but the final definition of a symbol should come from you yourself.

Each symbol you receive is unique and something that you can build on over the years. You may want to start a symbol dictionary of your own but if you find it too much effort with little payoff don't feel that you have to keep it up.

Psychic Protection

Before we discuss how to actually develop your psychic abilities (spoiler alert - yes you already have psychic abilities I'm just going to give you some workouts to strengthen them), I want to take a moment and talk about psychic protection.

This is one of those topics that is pretty important but not something to really be afraid of. Here is where I tell you - yes there are some scary and icky energies and entities out there - but they are nothing to really be frightened of, especially if you take precautions and understand how to protect your personal energy.

We are going to skip the high level metaphysical discussion about how none of these energies are really real and that you have just projected them through your mind because…for what people at our current vibrational level experience, they sure do feel real so it is good to have some protection techniques against them.

One "secret" of the metaphysical world is that you are immensely stronger than you think you are. The goal is to not give away your power and instead realize that nothing can or will hurt or disturb you if you set firm boundaries. You are in control of your energy. Protect it, control it, and you will be fine.

All the methods I am going to discuss use the basic principle of energy and vibrations. Your mind has the power to change the vibratory frequency around you just as different items in your household have different frequencies. Science is starting to catch up to this vibrational theory of reality that has been practiced for centuries by mystics and now just labeling and categorizing techniques that are common and widely used. If you want to know more information on this I suggest looking into articles and books discussing the science of consciousness and the quantum field.

Okay, now let's talk about some ways to protect your energy because there are a variety of different ways that individuals use. The key is to pick what feels right for you and what works with your belief system and way of looking at the world. If something doesn't feel right, don't do it. If there is something else you prefer that I don't mention, go with that. At the essence and core of each of these methods is that they remind you that you have the power and control in any situation. And if you want, choose multiple methods (I do) and keep your energy nice and protected!

White Light

We are going to start with probably the most popular method that is very effective and one that I highly recommend to anyone doing psychic work or really just going about your day. It may seem too simple to be true, but, in reality, this technique is highly productive and there is a reason that almost every single book on psychic work will teach this method.

To put white light around you, all you do is see the image of a white light surrounding your body in your mind's eye. Sounds a little too simple right?!!

Well, we can add a little to this to help you actually reinforce the idea and make your bubble stronger and more protective.

Here is a little exercise you can do:

First, close your eyes and take a few breaths to center yourself and go into your body. Feel yourself calming down. Feel energy flowing down your spine, down your feet and out into the ground. See how far down you can push that energy.

Now feel yourself bringing energy up from your feet up through your legs, up your spine and into your heart. Keep that energy there.

Next feel your energy coming into the top of your head, down your neck and into your heart. Pull the energy in with your breath.

Now see those two energies as a ball of white light in your heart. Take your breath and push that energy out around your body. Feel and see in your mind's eye the energy as white light surrounding your body.

Some individuals may feel warmer at this point as the energy engulfs your body. You may feel a tingling sensation or nothing at all. In your mind see this white light as a bubble of protection shielding you from outside energies.

Once you practice this method a few times you will find that it is very easy and can be a quick method to do. Whenever you are feeling "off" or "scared" or that you need some protection, this is a great technique to do. When I used to work in an office with other people, I would do this in my car before getting out to prepare myself for the energies I might encounter. For empaths, this is also helpful to implement before going into any location that has a lot of energy aka people.

Prayer or Mantra

Another very effective method to help protect your energy is to say a prayer or a mantra. This method also works well with the white light method and many times people combine the two. Setting your intention for protection and to be raised to a place of love will help you to keep your energy free of any negativity.

Any prayer that you feel called to will work, as long as you believe it and it works with your mindset. The Lord's Prayer or a few Hail Mary's are wonderful tools. Both have high vibrations and help raise the energy of the individual saying them.

Mantras are also great tools and if you have one that you are drawn to I would recommend using that. Personally, I use the mantra "May all beings be happy" or "Sabbe Satta Suhki Hontu" to center my energy and bring myself to a higher level that offers protection.

Additionally, you may find it helpful to come up with your own mantra or prayer to say before you engage in any psychic work. Something that sets your intentions for the work you are going to do and that you would like to be protected during that work.

Any of these methods work well for protection and you can use them in combination with each other or separately. Again, this is all about what works best for you.

Sacred Smoke

Sacred smoke is another one of those methods that has been used for years and in various cultures to offer protection to individuals. Perhaps the most widely used smoke for protection and cleansing being used nowadays is that of a smudge stick or sage. It has become so used and a symbol of the New Age community that sometimes I think people forget that it is actually a powerful tool.

Sage bundled together in a smudge stick or loose-leaf sage work wonderful to cleanse the air in the space you are located. If you feel a heavy or negative energy is in an environment this tool is effective to clear that energy out. I find that using it as a preventative measure to prepare the environment you are using for readings is also helpful as it discourages negative energy from settling in that environment.

This is not the only method or smoke that works to purify the energy or environment you are in. I have also found frankincense and myrrh to be a great tool to protect working spaces. You may even recognize different traditional religious organizations use this as well.

You can also pick an incense that you feel drawn to or even change it up for different types of work you do. When I first started this work, I tried out a variety of different incenses to see which vibration I preferred and what worked best for the type work I do. I even use different incense for different tasks depending on what I want to accomplish.

Crystals

Crystals have seemed to become ubiquitous in the metaphysical and New Age community and there is a good reason for that. Crystals emit vibrations that help to change the nature and field of the environment you are in. Some crystals are also well known to help protect the energy or field of individuals.

You will usually find that crystals that offer more of a protective quality are dark colored in nature, normally black. There are a variety out there and this is another case in which you want to try out some or hold different specimens and see what feels right for you. In the end, it doesn't matter what any books says or even what I write here, what works for you personally and what you feel drawn to will always be best.

In general, some popular crystals to use for protection include black tourmaline, smokey quartz, obsidian, and jasper.

You can place crystals in the environment in which you do your psychic work, or some individuals like to wear crystals in jewelry or carry them as pocket stones. Again, broken record here, do what feels right for yourself.

Another tip I have for finding crystals is to look to see if there are gem and mineral shows around you. If you are in a big city there is a chance that there may be one of these shows that happen once or twice a year. You will usually find more variety and lower prices at these shows then in traditional metaphysical stores. I have watched over the past decade as the prices of these stones have increased as interest has, and price gouging is something to look out for.

Candles

Candles are another great protective tool that have been used throughout the years and they are also pretty easy to come by. Candles provide fire and the symbol of light. Light the white light method above, the use of symbolic candles shows a predisposition towards the "light" instead of the "dark".

You can use different colored candles for different types of readings or practices, and you can also choose between unscented candles and those that provide a fragrance. Some individuals even sell candles that contain crystals, herbs and prayer intentions already in them. Finding a pre-made candles with protective energies already imbued is a great idea or, even better, you can create them yourself.

Don't discount the plain white unscented candle though. Although it may look plain and boring, a standard candle with no additions can be a very powerful tool.

You may find that lighting a candle before you begin any work sets the intention for protection in your space and helps you to get into the correct mindset.

Talismans

The idea of protective talismans has been around for centuries but currently they are not very popular so not talked about often. A protective talisman is simply an item that has been imbued with the energy and intention to provide protection.

These can come in many different forms ranging from necklaces to items passed down from previous generations. You may feel a connection to an old trinket that your grandfather carried around or something he kept in his wallet. Using this as a talisman and asking that grandfather to provide protection can assist your energetic field.

What a talisman is or how you use it is incredibly varied and personal. This is typically not something you can replicate or profit off of, so you don't hear too much about it. You may find an item on the ground such as a stone or a penny that you feel drawn to and this may be your talisman. Keep your mind open and you may find a talisman coming into your life.

In essence, a talisman is a reservoir of collected energy. It is an item where you put your energy and expectation of protection into and that item then carries that protective quality with it. Basically, you expect that item to be protective, you transmit energetically protective energy to it, it holds that energy and thus provides protection.

Spellcraft

For those readers that have a witchy bent, creating a spell or even a mojo bag to use during readings may be helpful. Again, this just depend on what you are comfortable with and where your belief system is. Spellcraft works on the same metaphysical principles as the rest of these methods and are just different vibrations working off of each other.

Putting together a mixture of different herbs (mugwort, sage, lavender), crystals (smokey quartz, black tourmaline, obsidian), and oils (rosemary, sage, rose) in a bottle or bag and sealing it with candle wax (black or white) while saying a spell is a great way to protect your energy as well.

Again, witchcraft is very personal and picking the recipe of ingredients that feel right for you will create a stronger energetic shield for yourself. I recommend either coming up with your own spell or looking at a few different protection spells and creating something that works best for you and your energy.

What I Do Before a Reading

Okay, now that I have given you lots of different ways to protect your energy and told you a bajillion times to do what is right for you personally, I thought I would tell you what I do personally. Now, of course, I don't recommend that you do what I do, but I always find it helpful to see how different people implement these practices in the real world. It always helps me conceptualize how these methods can be used.

Let's just go in order and as I actually do use each and every one of these methods I listed above. Some I used every day and some I use sporadically.

You may easily guess that the white light method is one I use each and every day. I actually have developed a daily routine that includes using this method so that it just becomes a common practice for me that I don't even have to think about. Each morning when I shower, I put a white light energetic protection around me. That way I can go through my day with my energy shielded.

Since I find this method the strongest and since it is also super-duper easy to do, I also use this method before I do any readings as well. Putting myself in white light (and moving my energy) is just part of my reading routine.

Additionally, I will put myself (and sometimes my family members), in white light if we are going somewhere with a lot of people and energies. This is a very helpful to do before going into hospitals where energies can be (but are not always) intense. I also got into the routine of putting my daughter in a protective white light when she would go to school every day and I do recommend this for parents as well.

Next up, we have the prayer or mantra. I already let you know the mantra I use generally, but I also have a variety of different sayings I use to generally protect my energy and set my intention prior to readings. I use my "Sabbe Satta Suhki Hontu" mantra when I am in a situation where I feel my energy becoming invaded or I need to pull myself back into my body and reestablish my boundaries. It is kind of like my automatic shield that I use.

In the past I have also used both the Lord's prayer and Hail Mary's to set my protective field but for the last five or so years

I have used Unity Church's Prayer for Protection which helps guide both my intention and my energy. This has a great vibration to it and offers a nice grounding energy for my belief system and energy field. I use this prayer for protection each morning with my white light intention as well.

Prior to readings I have a saying I use to direct where I want my energy to connect with and how I want my energy to be utilized. I ask for the protection of my "team and tribe" which includes my guides, angels, past loved ones and ancestors as well as setting the intention that the information being received is in "love and light". I do not do this every day, just prior to most readings.

Next up is sacred smoke. Before doing readings, I will usually light a candle and burn both a sage smudge stick and a stick of frankincense and myrrh incense. This used to be something I did each and every time I did any sort of reading, but as I have progressed with my skill and abilities in protecting my field I find that this is not something that I necessarily need to do each and every time. Saying that, it is something I enjoy, so more times than not, I do this before readings, but it isn't necessary for me anymore like it used to be.

I am also a proponent of use a smudge stick and saging my house from time to time. I do not have a set day or time period where I do this, I just do it when I feel my space needs this. In general, my household is pretty calm but if there are intense emotions for any reason that is normally a good time to sage to make sure the energy dissipates. Also, after those in laws come for a visit, but I probably shouldn't admit that in writing.

As for crystals, I love them and have a bunch of crystals in the room I do the majority of my readings. For protection I have a very large piece of back tourmaline that is under my desk and I sometimes place my feet on during readings (no shoes or socks of course). I also have small pieces of black tourmaline on the door frame of my reading room.

I am in tune with the vibration of many crystals, so I also enjoy using pocket stones for protection or just in general depending on what I am doing that day. If I know I am going someplace with a lot of energy (aka hospitals) I tend to put a piece of black tourmaline or smokey quartz in each of my pockets. I am pretty energy sensitive and have found this, along with other measures, protects my energy.

And now that I am thinking about it, I also have a very large chunk of smokey quartz that I keep next to my bed on my nightstand. This piece was actually mined from a mine called "Dreamtime" so it felt like it was meant to be. Side note - a benefit of acquiring your crystals from gem and mineral shows is that occasionally you get to talk to the individuals who actually found and mined the crystal.

I mentioned above that I light a candle with my sacred smoke rituals, but sometimes when I am not feeling the need for sacred smoke, I will light a candle at the beginning of readings. I enjoy the ritual of lighting a candle and then blowing it out after a reading is finished to disconnect from the energy. I will use any type of candle that is around, but I prefer plain white unscented candles. But if someone in my family happens to get a candle as a present or there is one on sale, I will use those as well.

Now onto talismans. As I said these are very personal and you likely won't be able to replicate the one I use, but I will tell you what it is anyway. So, one night I woke up in the middle of the night with the image of a crest in red in my vision. This image was not in my mind's eye, but something I was actually seeing with my physical eyes. I quickly wrote down everything I could see, and the image eventually faded. The next day as I was googling trying to figure out the significance of this image, I found the exact crest available as a necklace through an Etsy store. The crest was called "Brave Heart" and I quickly bought it. The actual crest was part of a wax seal that had been stamped and put onto a chain to create the necklace and when it arrived it came with a red seal of the stamp.

See, very personal story there. So if you happen to wake up in the middle of the night and see a crest in your eyesight and then find that as a wax seal necklace on Etsy you can use that as a talisman, but otherwise you will likely just stumble on something that works for you. I wear my necklace 24/7 and find that it both connects me with my spirit guides and offers a protective quality to it.

Finally, let's talk about witchcraft and spellwork. I do not currently have any active spells (that I can think of) that I am using for my psychic work right now, but I have in the past. Years ago, I created a mojo bag that offered a protective quality and helped to raise my vibration. I would say a spell to activate the bag and it had a nice scent to it from the oils I used that would help set my mind in the proper frame.

If I felt my energy threatened or that I needed some energetic oomph to my regimen I would likely create another bag or bottle, but I am not currently feeling that. For me my other methods are working well enough that I don't feel the need for a spell, but I am not shy to use this method if needed. Of course, I have been known to store spell bottles around my space and then forget about them, so in all probability there could be a protection spell somewhere in my reading room.

There you have it, my exhaustive list of all the protective techniques I use. Yes, I do most of these daily, sometimes several times a day. They take less than a minute so there is no reason not to. Protecting your energy is important, especially when doing readings for other people or with items.

As you raise your vibration your energy becomes more susceptible to outside energies. Protecting it is simple. Remember, you have the power to establish firm boundaries in your space. You control what you allow into your energetic field. Personally, I believe your mind is your biggest asset here, so I always recommend using that first.

Getting into the Psychic Frame of Mind

A lot about being a psychic is just shifting your mind set to a different wavelength. Many people call it "raising your vibrations" but another way to think of it is just a shift in the frequencies that you are choosing to focus on, like changing channels on a tv.

This is easy for me to say, but it is difficult for our rational minds to really comprehend. How does one shift the frequency they focus on? For this, there are several different methods you can use to "get you in the psychic zone" and in the frame of mind to start receiving and interpreting psychic information.

Which of these methods is best for you will be very individualized and likely depend on which of your psychic functions is your strongest. If you find yourself pretty clairvoyant, try the visualizations first. If you are physical and feel energy, try the breath work or moving of energy categories. Or just give each method a try and see what works best for you.

Visualizations

Over the years I've practiced a variety of different visualization techniques that got me in the right frame of mind to do psychic readings, and I will provide a few for you to try here. In the beginning, I used these almost every time I did a reading and found them extremely helpful. Once I got used to doing readings it became easier for me to just "sense" and "know" when I was in the proper state, but until I got to that point, I did a visualization almost every time I did a reading.

Elevator Ride

A popular visualization to get yourself in the psychic frame of mind is to imagine yourself in front of an elevator. The elevator opens up and you step in. Pay attention to the inside of the elevator - what does it looks like, is the surface reflective or solid? What shape are the buttons? Use your mind to make the elevator yours.

Notice that the elevator shows that there are seven floors with seven buttons each corresponding to a chakra. The first button is red, then orange, then yellow, the green, then blue, then indigo and finally violet. The top violet button is lit up and that is where you will be going. Push that top button and feel yourself raising as the elevator rises and each button lights up. Feel the corresponding chakra system light up as the energy and elevator moves up to the top floor.

When you get up to the top, before the elevator opens, pose the question you want an answer to. There is always that brief moment when an elevator stops before the doors open, this is your time to say your question in your mind. When the doors to the elevator open you will step off and receive the answer to this question in whatever form it takes.

Special Place

Another trick a lot of psychics use is to create a special place in their mind to do their psychic work. Whenever they visualize this place it will be a like a cue to themselves that they are seeking psychic information.

This special place can be anything you like. If you are a nature-type person you can visualize yourself next to a stream or in a calm meadow and let that be your location you go when you want information. If you prefer to be located indoors, even in your mind, you can visualize a house or a structure. Houses are nice because you can then create yourself a chair and a big screen on a wall. You can ask that the clairvoyant images you get be projected onto the screen. You can even give yourself a remote and turn it on when you want to activate your psychic senses and off when you are done. A cozy way to get some psychic work done.

The what or location of the place really doesn't matter. It is simply a location in your mind that you can visualize yourself going when you want to receive psychic information. The more detailed you make it the better as this will give your mind something to focus on when setting yourself up for doing a reading.

This has the added bonus of helping your clairvoyant skills. Clairvoyance has a lot to do with visualization and the better you are at creating images in your mind the more detailed images you will receive. When creating your room or space you also feel what it is like to create an image instead of receiving an image which is helpful in discerning information.

Once you have created your special place ask for the information you want to be sent to you. If you made yourself a screen that is a great place to receive it or you might just see it show up in front of you if you are outdoors.

I have found that when I used this technique, I often ended up using environments and locations that I had made up in my mind previously from different guided meditations I had done over the years. A guided meditation to sit next to a creek bed or a guided meditation to create a house with different rooms. If you find these types of meditations and practices helpful to walk you through each step of creating your psychic spot, there are many of different resources available for free from videos to podcasts.

Door

Similar but a tad easier than creating your own special psychic place or taking an elevator ride is to just create a psychic doorway as I mentioned at the start of this book. You can imagine your door however you prefer, a wood door, a metal door, a door covered in vines, whatever suits you best. Then set the intention that when you open the door the information you are seeking will be on the other side.

All of these techniques have different strengths and weaknesses. It may be wise for you to try out one each time and see if it works well for you or if you prefer something different. The elevator technique is great at teaching you how to raise your vibrations, but it is helpful to know a bit about chakras to really get the full benefit out of it. The special place technique is great, but it requires you to create a whole environment in your mind which can be time consuming at first. Then the door technique is quicker but may not give your mind the distraction it needs to let psychic information through.

You may find that one technique works great for you in the beginning, but as you evolve and your ability to connect evolves you can switch to a different technique or style. Like I have said, I have used each of these techniques at one time or another, but currently I do not use any of them. See what works best for you but don't be afraid to change it up in the future.

Moving Energy

My main way to get into the "psychic zone" now is to move my energy up to a higher vibration. This is one of those things that psychics say but people who haven't really experienced this have no clue what they are talking about.

For me I work a lot with my energy and moving it throughout my body. I do this with the psychic protection exercises and using energy as a shield and I do this to enter my zone and receive information. This is also something that took time to understand and develop a sensitivity to. We really don't learn about energy moving and feeling what that feels like in traditional schools.

How I started developing this technique was simply to practice pulling in energy from the crown of my head and feeling it move down my body and out my feet. I then repeat the process brining the energy up from my feet and out my head. I usually start my work once the energy has moved out of my crown chakra and to a higher vibrational space.

If you don't understand what this means this is a great time to *fake it until you make it*. Just imagine the energy doing this. Pretend that you are sending energy out of your feet and see that energy growing roots in the ground like a tree. Then pretend that you are pulling energy up from those roots and it is traveling up your spine and out the top of your head. You may not actually feel the energy at first but after some time you may start to feel a subtle shift of vibrations and energy.

Another helpful technique is to use your breath to help focus your energy. You can breathe in as you pull energy into your body and then breath out as you release energy out of your body. The breath is a powerful tool and manipulating and using energy.

Now to get into my psychic zone I simply move my energy from its normal location which is generally in my face area up to the top of my head and push it out a bit. For me there are subtle shifts that occur when I do this that tells me I am in "the zone". These "tells" are going to be personal so what tells me I am ready to receive psychic information may not be the same for you.

Personally, I feel a warmth sensation on my left cheek which is my signal that my main spirit guide is there and ready. I experience a slight ringing sensation in my ears and my vision looks like there is some small black splotches, almost like a television screen that isn't receiving a station (or how they used to look).

You may not experience all these signs and that is perfectly fine. You will find the subtle cues you receive that you are in the zone the more you practice and experience it.

I've also found that the shift happens much quicker now than when I first started. Previously it would take five minutes or so to find myself in the zone and feel comfortable doing readings. Now it is almost instantaneous and sometimes I have to ask for the information to stop until I can get to my computer or a piece of paper to write it down.

Don't be discouraged if at first you aren't feeling anything. This all takes time. You are building a skillset that hasn't been taught to you. Working with energy in your body is not something that is generally taught in Western society.

If you are finding this idea of energy manipulation really difficult to understand and use, sometimes a good yoga class or tai chi instructor can help you understand and feel energy. Just be aware that not all yoga or tai chi classes are the same, especially in their Western form, but there are good teachers out there that understand energy and can help in this manner.

Closing It Down

Now that you have several techniques to help you get into the psychic zone, this is where you will spend your time while doing readings and receiving information. After you are done it is important to shut off your psychic abilities and cut any energetic connections you have created. It is important to shut down your energy so you don't go throughout your day receiving random information about the people around you or attracting any icky energy attachments.

I have come up with a preferred method to shut down my energy, but in general you need to find your personal way to do the following:
1) Cut any energy connections made to other people or entities

2) Thank any entities that assisted in the reading
3) Release any extra energy accumulated
4) Come back into your body and ground your energy

Cut any energy connections made to other people or entities

I always end a reading with cutting the energetic connections to my clients. This is just one reason I tend to forget what I learned or received during readings soon after doing them. I cut the connection so I am not continually pulling on the client's energy field and the spout of psychic information stops.

There are several ways you can cut this energetic connection. Some individuals like to picture an energetic chord running between you and the other person and then imagine scissors cutting that chord.

Personally, I do a cutting motion with my hands and say in my mind "I cut any energetic connections formed between me and X. X's energy is theirs and mine is mine". I then physically push their energy away from me and pull mine back to me with my hands. I then sweep my hands quickly over my aura and place them on the ground, releasing any accumulated energy.

I know, it sounds like a lot, but it is quick to actually do it.

Thank any entities that assisted in the reading

I find it polite and thoughtful to thank any entities you have been working with. I just find this helps establish a good relationship and I when I have repeat clients I am better able to connect and receive information because a trust has already been create between me and their guides (I primarily work with spirit guides but this works with any entities your work with).

My way of doing this (again, its personal so do what is right for you) is to place my hands together and put them in the prayer position over my third eye thanking the client's guides. I then bring my hands to my mouth and say I love them (I'm a big proponent of the love vibration). I then bring my hands to my heart and say Amen (a great vibration to end on).

After I am done thanking my client's guides or other entities I worked with, I also like to thank my "team and tribe" for the services they provided. Again, it is always a good idea to thank entities for their assistance and send them love and I do this to mine as well as my clients.

Release any extra energy accumulated

There are several ways to release any extra energy. I prefer sweeping my hands over my aura and removing and extra energy and placing it into the ground as I described after I cut the connections with my client's energy.

Another helpful and very easy method is shaking your hands and imagine any extra energy flying out of them. Washing your hands with cool water may work as well. If you watch any shows where psychic do readings you will see that they usually have their own way to release energy, even if they aren't aware, they are doing this. It usually involves some sort of shaking of their body to release anything that they picked up.

Come back into your body and ground your energy

The final step in the process is to come back into your body and be your mundane human self. If you have been doing readings for a while this step is pretty important because you don't want to go about your day floating around and not really present.

Any good grounding technique works well for this. I usually only do something formal and bigger for this step if I've been doing multiple readings for hours at time, otherwise I find it easy to come back to myself simply by blowing out the candle I have lit and checking my emails.

A quick and effective way to ground your energy is to picture the energy that you pulled up in your mind flowing back down your spine and out your feet. Let roots grow from your feet into the ground and feel yourself establishing a connection to the world.

When I've been doing readings for long periods of time these simple methods do not always work and I may need something extra to really ground my energy. A good grounding technique I like and have used in the past is to go for a walk, barefoot if at all possible. Both the physical activity of moving my body and my feet on the ground help to bring me back. In the winter my favorite way to ground myself is to eat dark chocolate. I highly recommend that way.

What is most important with any of these techniques is coming up with your own plan that works for you and your time constraints. Be honest with yourself. Which part of the process are you going to spend time doing and which are you going to skip? I highly recommend always putting up a protective shield and other than that, have at it.

Psychic Exercises

Okay, you know the basics of how psychic abilities function, what they look like and a few ways to protect yourself. Are you ready to actually do some exercises to help strengthen your psychic muscles??

Using the analogy of your psychic abilities as muscles and doing "workouts" to enhance them seems pretty cliche, but it is actually a really great way to compare what it is you do. Most everyone is born with some sort of muscles, just like everyone is born with psychic ability. Sometimes as a kid you develop those muscles just by playing and having fun, and you do the same with your psychic abilities.

Psychic abilities in young children are generally strong and they don't have to "work" at it as much as adults. But as we age, we become more sedentary, letting our muscles fade and also adhering to the cultural norms that the world exists within the confines of our five senses. It takes time and effort either at the gym or in your home to build up muscles by doing exercises repeatedly, and the same thing is true with psychic abilities. It takes time and exercises to be able to perceive the world around you in a different manner.

Also similar to exercising, you can develop your psychic abilities alone or with a few friends working together. In some respects, working with friends is more fun and can be a very rewarding experience. Friends help keep you motivated and provide you immediate feedback. You will find many psychic development books out there that will give you a variety of exercises you can do with friends or groups of people to help you build your psychic abilities.

But…this isn't one of those books. I prefer to exercise alone just as I prefer to develop my psychic abilities alone. When I was working on building my own intuitive muscles, I would repeatedly get frustrated over all the exercises that required partners or someone else who also wanted to develop their abilities. If you have a friend that wants to do this with you - great! - but I am realistic in knowing that not all people have someone to do this with and even if you do, finding time to get together and practice may be difficult. You can always supplement the exercises I give you here with work with friends, but these exercises work perfectly well if you are by yourself or are highly introverted (like me!).

Enhancing Your Five Senses

Okay, so the first way we are going to start off developing your extra-sensory abilities is to focus on the senses that you do have and already know about. Sounds a little counter-intuitive right, but this method actually really works.

What I am talking about here is to slow down and pay attention to your physical senses - sight, hearing, touch (feeling), taste, and smelling. I would recommend taking one sense a week and really honing in and focusing on that physical sense.

Caveat before we begin - if you do not have the ability to use one of these senses, no big deal! You may already be ahead of the game and have developed another sense beyond its normal capabilities. So even if you can't hear very well, you may find that you can already sense vibrations (even if unconsciously) and know when people are going to come into a room.

The first week you can start with your sense of sight. When you go about your day to day activities take an extra moment here and there and really look around your environment. What do you notice? Can you see the individual grains in the texture of the wood floor? Can you see how the edge of a leaf is defined against the backdrop of the sky? Really pay attention to your environment and what is around you.

As you go about your week you may start noticing things you never realized where there or you aren't even sure how to categorize. Those leaves against the sky - do they have a sort of radiance or aura to them? When you look at a white wall do you see some fuzziness or energy vibrations coming off them? By paying attention to your environment and noticing the small things you will soon begin to notice things you have been discounting or not even realizing that they are there.

The next week you will want to focus on your sense of hearing. Can you hear the wind blowing through the trees? Does it sound different one day to the next or from one tree to the next? Does the hum of your computer sound a particular way? Is it different than the hum of your supervisor's computer?

Again, pay close attention. If you are a musician this is a great exercise to use to work on hearing different instruments in a song or picking out what notes or chords the guitar is playing in your favorite riff or song.

Towards the end of the week you may start to notice a buzzing noise in your ear at certain times of the day. You may also notice that your ears feel different ways and hear differently depending on the time of day.

I think you are getting the point here, right?

I would likely pick the sense of touch or feeling next. I am going to expand this to feeling instead of just touch because I want you to pay attention not only to what you feel with your hands but your whole body. Remember your skin is your largest organ and covers your entire body, not just your hands (I hope you know that skin covers your whole body…).

Anyway, pay attention to what different surfaces feel like. How soft is that blanket you use when you snuggle on the couch? How rough is the surface of your steering wheel? What does the air conditioning or heat feel like against your skin? Can you feel the vibration of your boss walking down the hallway before they knock on your door?

Focusing on your sense of touch and feeling is important because we haven't really been taught to focus on the vibrations around us. Waking up our hands and body to sensations will help you to notice the energy coming off different objects. After some time focusing on this sensation, pick up on object and see if you can feel the vibrations coming off of it. No big deal if you don't feel anything different, but you may be surprised to feel a pulsing or even tingling sensation from certain objects.

If you want, you can combine the sense of smell and taste the same week or separate them if you are extra sensitive. Let's be honest, if you get to week four and are still doing these exercises, you can totally combine them into one week. But if you are a purist and want to separate them out go for it.

Paying attention to your sense of taste can be an adventure and may even change what you eat. Take your time with the food you ingest, paying attention to any subtle tastes you experience. You may find that your favorite chocolate actually isn't that great and there is a reason good chocolate is more expensive (guilty of finding this out myself). When noticing your sense of smell try to pick up the different senses you encounter throughout your day. Can you pinpoint what the fragrance your usual bus driver wears reminds you of? What smells bring you comfort?

If you want, you can add on an extra week to work on recognizing your emotions. This may be pretty easy for some people but for others this can be a challenge. In particular, pay attention to where you feel the emotion in your body. Does anxiety tighten your chest, or does it feel like a bowling ball in the bit of your stomach? What does joy feel like? Sadness? This can be a helpful exercise in realizing when you feel certain ways and even when you do not realize you may be experiencing a certain emotion. Once you learn what your emotions feel like in your body you can them pick up when the emotions you are feeling are actually your own or if you are picking up and experiencing the emotions of people around you.

With any of these exercises you can either scatter them throughout the day or do them at one point. You can choose to pay attention to what you see at random intervals in your day or at a scheduled fifteen-minute session during a break in your otherwise hectic day. Do what works for you. If you have trouble remembering to do this exercise just set a timer to remind yourself or pair the activity with something you do every day like eating lunch or dinner.

What these activities do is help you realize that your innate senses are more than you really pay attention to. You filter out a lot of the information that your physical senses receive which means you also are not paying attention to your psychic senses. Taking time to strengthen your physical senses will also strengthen your psychic senses along with them.

These are pretty easy exercises you can continue to do throughout your life to hone your abilities. It also helps you realize how much of your life you live on autopilot and there are so many beautiful sights, sounds, tastes, smells, sensations and emotions that you can experience if you just pay attention.

Whose Name Is It?

This is one of my favorite exercises as it really works those intuitive muscles. For some it may seem intimidating at first, but it is likely you are just doing this by yourself alone in your room, so no one is going to know if you get the answers wrong or not - no big deal right! Trust yourself and allow yourself to just have fun. Being wrong is part of the learning process here - give yourself points for being wrong because it means that you are trying.

Okay, so what is this game that I'm talking about here? Well, it is all about learning how to read people, animals, or places. Basically, it is an opportunity to learn how you pick up and interpret psychic information along with strengthening those abilities.

I do this exercise two ways. One I call the "envelope game" and use envelopes and the other I call "names in a bowl" and use a bowl. Basically, you can do this exercise either way and it all depends on what resources you have around (aka do you own extra envelopes) and how likely you are to cheat and take a peek.

This is what you need to do. First, take a piece of paper and cut (or tear - if you don't have scissors) it into small one by three-inch pieces - or whatever size you get, it doesn't really matter, just make the piece of paper into smaller pieces of paper. On each of these pieces of paper I want you to write the name of a person, an animal, or a place.

The options are endless on what you can write on these pieces of paper by I have a few suggestions. First, in terms of people, try to only use people you know and that you are pretty sure wouldn't mind you reading them. If your mother is strongly against all things paranormal and it goes against her life philosophy, respect that and don't write her name down. If your sister loves reading her horoscope and talks about the latest deck of tarot cards that came in the mail, she probably wouldn't mind. Use your own discretion here and be ethical about it. You're eventually going to need to establish your own ethics involving psychic readings (we will talk about this later) so it is good to start now. If you get any anxiety about this, you can always ask permission of the person to use them in this exercise.

Along the line of people you are writing down, in addition to individuals you know in your life you may think about adding the names of celebrities but I have some warnings here. First, think of the ethics involved on whether or not you feel okay about reading them without their permission. Second, you need to be aware of how much celebrity culture is manufactured. When the media does an article about Celebrity A dating Celebrity B, it is highly likely that this is a

PR (public relations) stunt. Reading celebrities' true selves is difficult because you don't always know if you are picking up on the actual individual or just their **PR** personality and it can get confusing to tell the difference. And then you also have the ethical consideration of psychic spying on individuals that may be hiding aspects of their personal lives. Yes, there are many celebrities that have secrets that may not be appropriate to expose. So, check yourself and your ethics if you choose to use celebrities in this exercise.

For locations that you are reading, I would highly suggest using places that you know and that have good feelings associated with them. This means not doing a reading on the highly haunted Winchester house of the old church that is falling down a town over. Pick places that are nice or have a good energy to them.

Once you have a bunch of names, places and even animal friends written down on these pieces of paper, you can either fold them and put them in a bowl or place each one in a separate envelope. It doesn't matter how many of these items you write down but try to think of enough that you can't eliminate them from your mind and guess. I would say at least seven, but more is always great.

If you are using a bowl, make sure to fold the pieces so they don't open up when you reach your hand in - this is where you want to pay attention to your personality and decide which way will work best. Are you the type of person who will cheat and take a peek? If so, using the envelope system where you put one piece of a paper in each envelope will prevent that cheating process or at least make it more difficult.

Now, when you are ready for this exercise, get into your psychic zone. Put up your psychic protection and raise your vibration to a place where you feel ready to access your intuitive abilities. Create your psychic doorway or go on your elevator up to the top floor. Do whatever you want to do to be the psychic you know you are.

Take one envelope or slip of paper out of the bowl. You can place the piece of paper under your non-dominant hand and have a pen or pencil along with a blank piece of paper in your other hand. In your psychic zone see if you can pull any information from the name or place. Write down any and all impressions you get, even if they feel reckless. You can also label if you feel like you are using your intuition or your logic when different pieces of information come up.

With this activity I like to give it at least five "touches" before I give up and take a look. This means I connect to the psychic energies and see what comes up five different times. Pay attention here, you may get images in your mind, words or songs, a taste in your mouth, a gut feeling - whatever it is, write it down.

If you are having trouble picking anything up psychically, try asking questions. What does this item look like? What does this item smell like? How does it feel? Is this a person, animal or building? Does it have masculine, feminine or neutral energy? Start asking a few questions and see if that leads you anywhere.

You can repeat this activity with a few more slips of paper or envelopes or, if you are impatient and want to know how you did you can just check and see if you are right or wrong. Try to pay attention to what information was a 'hit" and what that felt like. Did that information come to you before you even grabbed the piece of paper? Did you feel like you needed to peel back a layer to get to that information? Did the information that was wrong feel different? Did it feel like you were trying to rationalize who it was? Did asking questions to yourself help or hurt you - did it knock you out of your psychic zone or were you able to maintain it while asking the questions?

This exercise is a good way to both strengthen your psychic ability and to figure out which areas are your strong suits and which aren't. I find it very helpful to write a lot of names and places down at one time and then use the same bowl of names until I get through them all. This way I usually forget who or what I actually wrote down so my logical mind can't butt in too much. I just leave the bowl in a safe location where I do most of my readings and then come back to it from time to time to practice this skill.

Remember, no one is watching you do this exercise and the point is to learn more about yourself and your abilities. Let yourself try this and don't judge yourself too harshly. Getting the wrong information is just as helpful as getting the correct information because it tells you what that feels like as well.

Psychometry

Psychometry is the art of receiving psychic information from holding items of an individual. This is like the bread and butter of psychic work and is why you will see a lot of psychics and mediums on television shows asking if an individual has any items that they can hold. It forms a connection to another person instantaneously and sometimes makes it easier to read their energies.

I'm going to be honest here. I personally do not practice much psychometry, and this is mainly because I do the majority of my work at home by myself in a room and over the internet. Instead of using an object to form a connection or "anchor" with an individual I use a name. Perhaps that is why I like the previous exercise so much, because that is the type of connection that works the best with the work I do.

With that said, learning and practicing psychometry is a great exercise for anyone to do to strengthen and hone their psychic skills. You may find that it works better for you to gather information using objects than just people's names. And it is pretty simple. All it requires is an object...and maybe someone who knows something about that object to verify your findings.

I can't really think of a legitimate way to practice this exercise at your house, by yourself, without a friend (probably why I don't do this type exercise regularly), but if you have a person who is willing to let you hold some item from some long deceased ancestor or a family member and see what you get - go for it!

You can also go to antique or secondhand stores and try reading items they have for sale. One caveat I have with this method is that you can unknowingly start reading the energy of someone who was very negative or did not have a peaceful life or death, so you want to make sure your psychic shields are fully up before doing this. It will also be nearly impossible to verify your findings on items just sitting on the shelf at an antique store.

In general, items that are made of metal and are hard tend to hold energy vibrations best. Fabrics can work but if they have been washed or are too old, they may be difficult to read. Books are hit or miss whether you can pick up energy off of them.

If you have the opportunity and means to practice psychometry, go for it. You just hold the item in your hand, get into your psychic zone, and see if you receive any information. Some people prefer using one hand to another, so you might want to switch it up and see if you get more information with one specific hand. I recommend just trying this exercise if you have the opportunity and see if it works for you.

Increasing Clairvoyance

Doing exercises to strengthen your psychic abilities doesn't have to feel like work. You can use your normal everyday hobbies and activities to actually increase your ability to see and perceive images in your mind's eye. You can also have some fun and make yourself laugh in the process!

These exercises are not activities that involve actually connecting with your psychic center. Instead they are activities that help strengthen your clairvoyant abilities and allow the images you receive to be clearer, last longer, and be easier to spot.

Read fiction...better yet, listen to audiobooks

Perhaps my absolute favorite way to strengthen my intuitive insight is to read fiction. When you read a book, you create scenes in your head of what the characters look like and the amazing places they travel. A good writer can make you feel like you are in the scene – you can touch what the character is touching and taste the exotic foods they eat.

Even better than reading, I find that audiobooks allow my eyes to lose focus and get into the trance like state they tend to find when activating my clairvoyance. Audiobooks also allow me to practice focusing on clairvoyant images when I am doing something else – out grocery shopping or for a daily walk. This way, when I receive information in situations where I am not at my desk, I can realize it for what it is and pay attention.

The trick with this tip is to find a genre that you can really get into. Don't shy away from books that seem don't seem "cultured" or "erudite". Yes, you can do this exercise while listening to Pride and Prejudice (for that I recommend Audible's version – the narrator is great!) but you can also do this while listening to 50 Shades of Grey (I'm just using this as an example, there are much better romances out there – just try anything by Penelope Douglas). Find a book that you can get into and then let your third eye take over!

Create scenes in your head

I was developing and strengthening my third eye before I even knew what a third eye was. From the time I was a child, I enjoyed creating scenarios in my head and immersing myself inside them. These could be anything from wishes for the future or walking through what the next day would bring. I would take the time right before I fell asleep and just let my mind get pulled away.

This practice is a great way to work on both your manifestation skills and your intuitive work. The more energy and emotion you put behind imagining what you want to manifest, the more you are working with universal forces to let that happen.

With this exercise try to see how detailed you can get the image. If you want a new kitchen in your house, try to imagine the exact feel of the countertops or the specific hue of the paint color. If you have an ideal vacation in mind, try to see in your mind's eye each step of the journey, from checking in at the airport to exploring an abandoned castle.

This is another exercise that is fun and practical on multiple levels.

Change people's appearance when you meet them

How many times have you been introduced to a person and then can't remember their name the next time you see them? I know I sometimes don't even try because I know how bad I am with names – I can remember their energy and feeling I receive from them but not what name they told me.

A fun trick you can use to remember someone's name and strengthen your intuition at the same time is to add intuitive images to their appearance in your mind's eye when you meet them.

Say you meet a nice young lady named Robin. Simply imagine a robin on their shoulder while you are talking with them. Or perhaps the gentleman's name is Richard. You can picture your uncle Richard's face superimposed on top of the individual or even give the guy a second head.

This exercise is also a good one that allows you to strengthen your intuition while doing something else – while talking with your eyes open in a location that is not preset. Doing this allows you to become more aware of information coming in when the setting isn't perfect.

And you don't have to just reserve this exercise for those whom you don't know their name. Perhaps you have an annoying manager at work – give them devil's horns or a lion's tail the next time you see them. At least you can entertain yourself while they are talking with/at you.

Meditate with images

Another practical way to strengthen your intuition is through meditation. Yes, everyone and their mother is talking about meditation these days – and I have varying opinions on its necessity or technique. But the truth is, if you are going to meditate anyway, this is also a great time to work on strengthening your clairvoyant skills – especially if you get easily distracted during typical meditations. There are a variety of ways to do this.

First, you can use a guided meditation that will walk you through different scenes that you can imagine in your mind. This will help you to develop new locations and situations that you might not have thought to experience on your own – kind of like an audiobook but with a focus on relaxation or spiritual work. Check online as there are many of these available for free in different forms, from podcasts to YouTube channels.

Another way I like to use this skill is in just a standard meditation when you follow your breath in and out. Instead of just going blank in my mind, sometimes I like to take control and picture images, especially if my mind is highly busy and active at that time, not wanting to settle down. My favorite image that I tend to go back to is that of the ocean waves going in and out. I set my breath to the waves and see them, in full detail, going out towards a sunset and back in towards the beach. If you want, you can also imagine the smell of the beach and the way the water feels hitting your feet as it comes in and out to activate more psychic senses. This has the benefit of being extra relaxing as well!

Using Divination Tools

Tools to access your psychic intuition are very popular, but a lot of time people forget that their original purpose is to make you aware of your own psychic intuition and they end up depending more on the tool more than their own insights. Now, these tools that I am talking about are basically any form of divination that you can think of from cartomancy to runes.

Using divination tools is a great way to have an external manifestation of your internal psychic abilities. They can be used sort of like a crutch to get you used to your intuition or they can also be used to enhance your intuitive insights.

I recommend picking one tool to start out with and then expanding from there if you find that you enjoy using these props. Some popular divination tools include tarot, pendulums, runes, or even astrology. The important thing is to stick with one method until you understand it to such a degree that you allow your intuitive insight to superimpose itself on top of the given tool. Spending your time looking up the meaning of a tarot card or an astrological aspect is going to hamper your intuitive insights, but if you know the meaning right away you leave room for your intuition to also have a say.

I have used all these methods throughout the years, and I do not find one better than the other, it is all a matter of preference and what you are drawn to. If one of these tools is calling your name, pick it up and see where it leads you.

Tarot

Tarot cards are a great tool for those who have strong clairvoyant abilities as they also rely on pictures and symbolism to get messages across. If you want to learn more about tarot and how to use the cards my personal recommendation is to get and read one really great tarot book and then stop there. Many people spend years buying more and more books and reading about tarot instead of actually practicing tarot and tuning into their own abilities. It will be much better time spent laying cards on the table and doing a reading rather than going over your twelfth tarot book. Of course, I would recommend checking out The Only Tarot Book You'll Ever Need (hint - I co-authored that book), but there are some other great books on the market to get you started including Rachel Pollock's 78 degrees of wisdom and Tarot Plain and Simple by Anthony Louis.

Pick a book that you feel drawn to and use that as a resource to get you started, but then don't forget to put it down and actually use the cards. You will soon learn to trust your intuitive hunches as to what a particular card means in a given situation and not depend on the definition provided in any book.

With the cards, you may find that you start to have clairvoyant visions after you ask a question while shuffling or laying out the cards. You may find words or phrases coming into your mind while you are describing what each card means. Being open and aware of your own psychic abilities will assist you in reading an understanding the cards.

Pendulums

Pendulums are super simple tools for Individual's to get started using. These are great for people who are energy focused and sense or experience energy deeply. A pendulum is basically just an item on a string that will move in a certain direction to answer whatever question you ask. These have been around for centuries and can be as simple as a ring attached to a string or a crystal attached to a chain.

When using a pendulum, you will ask a question and then pay attention to which direction the pendulum swings. It may swing clockwise, counterclockwise, diagonal, up and down, or left and right. What each of these movements mean is specific to you personally, so figuring out that ahead of time, sometimes called "programming" your pendulum is important. Basically, you just ask your pendulum to show you what yes, no and maybe look like and then go from there.

Pendulums are also sensitive to energy and can be used to check chakra states or determine the predominant energy in an individual. They can also be helpful to check the psychic impressions you are receiving to understand if they are correct or not. One drawback is that Pendulums really only answer yes or no questions, but you can use them as a good back up when you are having trust issue with your own intuitive abilities.

Runes

Runes are good if you are a history buff or into mythology and also work great with those whose predominant sense is clairaudience. Runes are simply stones or items with letters of the runic alphabet drawn or engraved onto them. There are a variety of different languages that can be used and different methods in which Individuals utilize this tool.

Out of all the tools I'm discussing here, runes are the one that I have used the least, so my knowledge base is not as wide as with the other tools. Many people use runes in divination similar to tarot by drawing a specific number of runes for different questions and then interpreting based off what the symbols mean, however, there are a variety of other methods that are also used to divine with runes.

When working with runes, you can use your intuition to tell you how the rune's meaning fits the question in hand or if any additional information can be added from insights you receive. Because the runic alphabet is different from most individual's common language, the change in words spoken and heard can sometimes activate your clairaudience. You are not likely to hear the rune names spoken throughout your day so when one pops in your mind it is something to take note of and be aware of. These runes may come into your mind when a question is asked, or you may hear the names of runes to describe people you meet.

Astrology

Astrology is a great tool for those interested in doing a lot of learning and research. It is also wonderful for those who are claircognizant as a lot of astrology has to do with going with what you just know.

Out of all divination methods, astrology likely contains the most time required for "book learning" as the subject is vast and covers many thousands of years. There are also a variety of different types of astrology that you can learn including the simple method of reading an individual's natal chart (the chart of where the planets where at the moment of their birth) to understand their personalities, seeing how transits (where the planets currently are in the sky) are effecting an individual or situation, or horary astrology or predictive astrology where you pull a chart when a question is asked and use it to get the answer to name a few.

What all the methods require is a lot of study and understanding. You need to know what the planets mean, how the different signs affect them and what they represent in the different houses. Throw in interactions between the planets (known as aspects), all the points on the chart that are important (midheaven, ascendant, and others), and a myriad of other mathematical points on a chart (nodes, part of fortune) and you have a lot of information that takes years or even decades to understand.

If you are willing to put in the time and effort, you will find that your intuition starts to lead you into what transits or planets are actually important and what they actually mean. It just takes a while to get to that point when the astrological information comes so swiftly that it does not impede the intuitive side.

Once are familiar with astrology pay attention to that feeling of just knowing which planet is the most important one in someone's chart. See if one transit that an individual is going to experience just feels more important than the others. When you understand what all the pieces of a chart mean you can then let your psychic abilities have free rein to get a deeper reading on a chart.

Connecting to Plants and Animals

One of my favorite ways to train my psychic skills in a safe and ethical manner is to work with connecting to plants and animals, the natural world around you, instead of actual people. When connecting to people you always need to be cognizant of their potential energy and your ability to protect your own energy against any yuckiness you may encounter. But plant and animal life are generally "cleaner" in their energy and they project and are surrounded by it in a similar manner as humans.

You can connect to the natural world in the same way you do people. There is no difference there. Use your anchor to draw the energy to you and then use your abilities to read what their energy tells you.

One drawback in this exercise is that you won't necessarily be able to get confirmation what you are receiving, but sometimes you may surprise yourself by getting information that you can find an external validation for.

Perhaps my favorite story about connecting to an animal energy is when I was training to be a medium (an individual who communicates with those who have passed away). During one of my sessions I connected with an entity I thought was a friend of the individuals who had passed away in their teens and had red hair. I received information about a favorite toy, their name, and what they enjoyed doing. Little did I realize that I was actually connecting with a golden retriever! The energy came through so strong and clear that I thought I was communicating with a person and not a pet!

I tell that story just to assure you that connecting to animals is possible and sometimes it can even be difficult to distinguish an animal energy from a person. There is a whole subset of psychics who main area of focus is as animal communicators. If you are looking for practice and don't have people to practice on, try your family pet or your favorite tree in the park!

Psychic Apps

Many times, in the psychic and metaphysical community, there is a stress and emphasis put on connecting with nature and eschewing technology. I feel, however, that there is a time and place for technology, and it isn't something that should be outright dismissed. You can use your phone as a psychic tool just as well as you can use a deck of cards or the shapes of clouds in the sky.

Recently, there have been a number of apps added to the market that actually are designed to help train and enhance your psychic abilities. I recommend a search of whatever app store you prefer to see what is available and interests you.

Currently, two of my favorite apps include ESP Trainer and RV Tournament.

ESP Trainer is an app that you can use whenever you have a few minutes of extra time. The basis of the app is that you have four color blocks to choose from with a picture being "hidden" behind one of the blocks. Each round you have 24 tries to see how many times you can figure out where the picture is hidden. Don't expect to get all 24 or do if you are good at this type of activity, as the app says to contact them if you repeatedly get more than 12 right.

In contrast to ESP Trainer, RV Tournament is an app that you use once a day. In this app you are given a number that designates a picture. You use your psychic abilities to read what the image looks like then, after doing this, you are given two images to choose between based on your findings. Then you wait until the next day to reveal if you got the image right or wrong. This is a highly simplified description of a more advanced app, but as of me writing this, this app is the best I have found at giving you an objective object to "read" and practice your psychic abilities.

If you have an interest and these apps are currently available, I highly recommend downloading them…especially because they are free so you can try without any cost to you.

Technology is advancing rapidly and by embracing using it we as psychics can find benefits to increasing and utilizing our abilities. This isn't the only way I use technology in my work, and I bet in the future there will be many more ways to integrate technology and psychic abilities.

When Things Go Wrong

One thing outsiders always like to criticize and use against psychics is when they get information wrong. When they say something is likely to happen on a certain date in a certain way and then it doesn't happen. This can be frustrating for professional psychics who know how energy works and also disheartening to those in training when they don't get verification of what they believed would happen.

There are a variety of different reasons that this can happen, and we are going to explore a few. Along with that, we are going to talk about what happens when you just draw a blank, no information coming in on a subject you are trying to read or when your information is so off the mark it isn't even close to being right.

The most important thing to remember when things seem to go wrong is to not give up hope. Believe in yourself and keep putting yourself out there. You will soon learn to trust your psychic senses just as much as you trust your physical senses.

Why Psychics are Sometimes Wrong

I like to think that I am a pretty decent intuitive. I do readings
for people from across the world and have provided some great
insight to individuals who I will never meet in person. I also
give myself daily readings and tend to follow my own advice –
so I like to think that that advice and information is good.

But you know what, sometimes I am wrong.

I know, I know, that is hard to admit, but it is the truth. Any
psychic or intuitive that tells you they are right 100% of the
time either has a secret that the rest of the psychic community
doesn't know or is just not telling you the truth.

So why exactly are perfectly good and reasonable psychics not
always right? If we purport to tell the future, why do we get it
wrong sometimes and right others? Well, I have several
different possibilities for you to consider.

Wrong Information for a Greater Purpose

I have had guides tell me information that I knew wasn't
exactly correct, but I passed it along anyway because that is the
information that the guide wanted my client to know. Why is
this?? Sometimes when we are told something that is "wrong"
and we don't like it, it shakes us up. It changes our energy and
our focus so that we can then manifest into our lives something
that is even better.

Yes, sometimes guides will lie to psychics, but really, it is for
the best interest of everyone involved, so just roll with it.

And yes, it takes a recognition of your own self-worth as a reader to pass along information that you know isn't entirely correct and then not say that you know. You have to remove your ego to provide a great reading.

Energy is Fluid

There is a different reason why psychics sometimes get a reading wrong that has nothing to do with guides not being truthful and everything to do with how the universe works and probabilities.

Okay, so I am going to try to explain to you a little bit about dimensional realities without getting too much into the philosophy or quantum mechanics behind it. There is this "theory" (or reality, if you prefer) that every decision we make leads to the creation of a different probable dimension – realities that are occurring just as real as the one you are living right now. Just imagine that there are a bazillion other replicas of you out there living this life but following different paths.

There is the "you" that got into Harvard and is living the life of an investment banker in Philadelphia. There is the "you" who didn't turn down the job offer from the animal shelter and now spends their day petting homeless kitties. There is the "you" that dumped that high school boyfriend and is still single in New Jersey. All these replicas exist simultaneously but in different dimensions of reality.

Those might be some very extreme examples, but it gives you an idea of what I am getting at here.

Back to psychic readings. When we do these readings, we are trying to follow a line of probabilities to see what will most likely occur down the line. I sometimes see these probabilities as guitar strings, and you have to figure out which string is most likely to be plucked – which vibration or chord you are going to experience in this reality that we are currently in.

And, sometimes, you play a different string. Sometimes you zig when I thought you were going to zag. That doesn't mean that you didn't follow the string that I thought you were going to follow – it just means that that reality in which you did is not the one we are currently in.

Did I lose you there?

So, what I am saying is that, actually, I was right in that psychic reading, just I was right for a different probable self that you are currently not experiencing. And the farther out the prediction goes, the more difficult it is for a psychic to be completely correct. This is just how the metaphysical universe works.

Some People are Difficult to Read

Another reason you may find yourself having a difficult time getting correct information about a person is if they are a difficult read. Some people just feel like they are shoving information into your mind while others it feels like you are pulling it from every available crack.

There are a few reasons why some people are more difficult to read than others and most of this involves how they hold their energy and their belief systems.

I personally find hard core skeptics who don't believe in psychics or any sort of unseeable reality to be some of the most difficult people to read. It feels like they put up a block to information because they actively don't want their thoughts to be shown false. Because they have this mindset it can sometimes create an energetic barrier that makes it difficult to actually get to their energy and thus they are able to keep their mindset intact.

You may say, well, these are the type of people who aren't likely to get a psychic reading, but that is not always the case. These individuals may come to you with their arms crossed in front of them, most likely a friend or partner dragging them through the door. These individuals have something to prove, either to you or to the individual that brought them through that door - mainly that you are a fraud.

Another hiccup in these types of readings is that for some psychics, you will see their ego get involved in this situation as well. Yeah, sometimes that psychic wants to prove to the client that they are totally awesome and amazing – because, let's face it, they are! And guess what…the ego plane is a lower vibrational level and that is a state where that psychic won't necessarily get correct information. That psychic will end up using his/her imagination instead of their intuition. Yep, that psychic won't be able to "prove" to the hardcore skeptic that they are right…because they won't be.

But this does not mean that you can't be a skeptic and get a good reading. I am a skeptic about a lot of things. I need it proven to me before I can believe it. What is important is that I keep an open mind. That I allow my mind to change and transform based on the evidence that I see. That my mind is pliable and my energy open.

Ego

As I mentioned above, having your ego play a role in a reading is never a good thing. You will find that when you want to be right to prove something, that is normally when you end up being wrong. Being aware of your own ego and when you are acting from this level will help you to see when you should turn down a potential reading opportunity.

When you are operating from your ego, you are operating from a lower vibrational energy. You are basically reading a difficult chapter of a book. Yeah, you may be able to get some of the answers to the quiz correct, but not as well as if you were reading the chapter you were meant to read.

This is also one reason I caution people against doing readings for family and friends. A lot of time you want to prove to them that you are in fact psychic. You want them to recognize how cool and amazing this ability is. But when you try too hard in that area, you end up disappointing yourself.

It is important to remember when doing readings that you do not have anything to prove. That you are merely just an individual passing along the information you are receiving. Trust in yourself and your abilities will go a long way to proving readings that are correct.

Wrong Interpretation

Another reason you may find that a reading you did is not exactly correct is due to how you interpreted the information you received. I have heard various psychics and mediums that are prominent in the field say that what they receive is always correct, but how they interpret it may not be. I find this to be true as sometimes a lot can get misinterpreted between what something is supposed to mean and what you think it means.

As you do more and more readings you will start to develop a sort of vocabulary with the spirit world on what images mean. An image of a rose may mean love for you, but it may mean celebration for a different psychic. However, many times you are faced with a symbol that you have never seen or experienced before and interpreting what that symbol means may not always be easy.

Because of this, I like to do a reading for myself every morning, asking what energy I can expect. This is usually where I will receive new symbols that I then will understand what they mean as the day progresses. Sometimes I do some research to try to understand the symbol right away, and other times I just watch how the energy plays out.

I distinctly remember being taken aback one morning with the image of a white duck quaking in my face. I had no idea what that was supposed to mean, but the energy was so strong that I literally flinched at the image. Later in the day I would receive a very good offer and when I looked up what white ducks could symbolize, I saw that good luck was an option. So now whenever I see a white duck as a symbol I know to say "yes" to any opportunities that come my way that day.

But you can see from that example, that I could easily misconstrue the meaning of a white duck. Personally, when I think of a white duck the image from the white duck in the commercial for disability insurance comes to mind. On that day I could have thought that I or someone I know was going to experience some sort of minor accident that prevented them from working.

If this was for a reading and I gave this interpretation of a potential injury, I would have been wrong, but the information and image I received would have been correct. The image of the white duck is clearly there, it was just my interpretation of what that quacking duck meant that had the potential to be incorrect.

This is just one reason I like to describe exactly what I am seeing or hearing in a reading and then provide my interpretation of it. I also have a disclaimer in all my readings for the client to add their own interpretation because they may have a greater insight than I do on whatever I am seeing.

If you learn to trust the information you receive you will find that most of the time it is correct, just how you interpret those signs and symbols may need a little tweaking.

No Information

Probably one of the big fears when you are beginning to do psychic readings is that you won't pick up any information. Let me tell you a little secret. Once you release this fear and just trust you will soon realize that you will always receive information. Releasing the fear lets go of the block. The information and energy is always there, you just have to be open to read it.

But, until you get to that point, there are a few things you can be aware of and do when you suddenly come up with no information.

You may find that you read energy better at a certain time of day or during a particular time of the month than others. Yes, this may have to do with the moon, but there are actually studies that have been done with remote viewers (a type of psychic which became popular with the government) on if their menstrual cycle effects the accuracy of their readings and they have found a correlation. Paying attention to when you pick up a lot of information and when you come up blank may help you see if there is a pattern.

You may also find that sometimes your day to day reality make it difficult for you to get in the psychic zone. Focusing more on spirituality and occult topics can help raise your vibration and put you in the right mindset to pick up information. Also, just watching funny videos will raise your vibration - so if you are having trouble picking up psychic information, don't worry, just watch a silly cat video!

Try not to put too much pressure on yourself to get information. Especially early on in your psychic development process you may find that performance anxiety makes it difficult for you to tune in. This is one reason why a lot of my psychic exercises involve activities that can be done by yourself. The only one who is judging you is you. Take other people's opinions out of the picture and this may help you build confidence.

There are also times when you are just not supposed to know anything about a subject or that you client is not meant to know. During these times I actually receive information, but that information is typically in the form of a big bright white light blocking my view. Sometimes nothing is something - meaning sometimes not getting information is the information itself.

If you are truly feeling like you just can't pick up information on a person or subject, be honest and say something. It is okay to not get anything. It is okay to be wrong. Be honest with yourself and who you are reading for. Don't try to fudge information or push through when there isn't anything there. There may be a larger purpose reason that you just are not aware of as to why no information is coming through.

Psychic Tips

Now that you know what your psychic senses are and how to activate them, how about some tips on the process. Developing your psychic abilities isn't necessarily something that is going to happen overnight. I mean…it might for a few out there, but for others this is a process that is going to take months or even years to accomplish. Don't give up if you feel like you aren't receiving information at first. Keep up the practice and the effort and you will find information comes to you. I assure you, a little practice every day is all it takes to get you started on this journey of embracing your psychic abilities.

Ask

This sounds so simple, but this piece of advice is actually so important when you are learning to develop your psychic abilities. You need to ask your questions before you are going to receive an answer. Yep, sometimes just asking is what is needed.

Many times, people will wonder why they aren't receiving psychic information and think themselves not psychic because they don't know in advance that they are going to get in a confrontation with their boss or that their mother is going to call on a Tuesday. Well, did they ask about this information?

Yes, sometimes you will receive information out of the blue. You will get that gut feeling that says to go a different way to work and later learn that there was an accident on your normal route, or you will see the image of your sister in your mind minutes before she calls. But this isn't always the case. Sometimes you need to ask the question first.

Something that I have gotten into the habit of doing is to ask every morning what my energy is going to be like for the day. This way I get a general sense of what I can expect and look forward to. I wouldn't necessarily know this though if I did not ask.

Think about what questions you have about your life in general or just any mundane topic. Do you want to connect with a certain ancestor or hear from your spirit guide? Have you asked them to come forward? There really is no harm in just asking.

Using an Anchor

When doing a psychic reading it is often helpful to have what I call an anchor, or something to direct your psychic senses to the information you are choosing to read. Basically, you need to have something that connects you to the place in the energy field you are wanting to connect to. Think of an anchor like the reference number for a library book. Knowing this number makes it easier to find the correct book to read.

There are a variety of different things you can use to anchor the energy of a reading. As I discussed in the psychometry section, using an object can be a great way to anchor you into an energy. Using an object, you can both feel the vibratory energy off of that object and read the energy directly connected to the object. Sometimes events surrounding a particular object may be difficult to discern from the energy of the person that used the object meaning you may know of a violent crash that happened with a motorcycle helmet but have a difficult time reading the actual person who was wearing the helmet.

Another possible anchor many individuals like to use are pictures of individuals. When using a picture make sure that the person or place you are going to read is prominent in the image. Sometimes pictures with multiple people can be difficult to distinguish and sometimes it is easier to read the location the picture is taken or the emotions happening during that image than what is currently going on for that individual.

My personal favorite anchor to use is the name of an individual. I find this a great way to connect to a person's energy without needing to have any physical object. Names also carry vibrations in themselves so that can add another layer to a reading.

You do not need anything direct, however, to do a reading. Just a random number assigned to an image or a descriptive word associated with a person can also be used to anchor a reading. I have used email addresses like Vulcan545 or moonbeam28 that do not contain an individual's actual name to do readings because that is connected to their energy field. You can also use a nickname an individual prefers or any word they want to associate with their energy.

Individuals who do remote viewing tend to just use a number sequence which has been associated with a location or object. Many times, the numbers have no relation to a place and are completely random, but they still work to anchor a remote viewer into a specific location. Remote viewing is the use of psychic abilities to read locations, but the actual process tends to be very regimented since it was developed by the military. Through their tests they proved that you can read places and images with random number sequences. At the start they used actual coordinates of a location to remote view it, but later they switched to assigning random numbers like 6384-8679 to prove that the remote viewers were not cheating or could not be accessing long forgotten information in their conscious mind.

Whatever you choose to use to anchor your reading, you will find that having something to depend on is very helpful. What you use can always shift and change as you learn and develop so you may want to try a few different ways and see what you prefer. Having multiple possible anchors to work with is also helpful in case you come upon an individual who does not have or want to give you your preferred anchor. Meaning, if someone doesn't want to give me their actual name, I can still do a reading for them using their email or a randomly generated number.

Distracting Your Conscious Mind

Sometimes when you are doing a reading, you end up thinking too much and your mind becomes a problem. You may start questioning if the information you are receiving is correct or end up putting an energetic block in your own energy due to anxiety or worry as to if you will receive correct information.

A technique many psychics like to use is to distract their conscious minds while doing readings. There are many different ways to do this, but the ultimate goal is to let your conscious mind be occupied by something mundane and then allow your psychic mind to come through.

There are a number of prominent psychics and mediums who find scribbling on a piece of paper a very helpful method. This is also a pretty simple method because all you need is paper and a writing utensil. With this method you don't try to draw any images just make lines on a paper to give something for your conscious mind to focus on. This also allows you to have space to jot down any notes or information you may receive when tuning into an individual.

If you want to check out how this technique works, Tyler Henry had a show called "Hollywood Medium" where you could watch him scribble on a piece of paper while doing psychic and mediumship reading celebrities. He is also a great example of someone who spent years training his abilities. Even though he is very young, he did put in the time and effort to build up his intuitive muscles and it is very apparent.

Other psychics find items that you can hold, such as crystals or talismans helpful. You can hold a small crystal and move it around in your fingers to keep your mind occupied. I like to

think of this like a psychic fidget tool, just something to help
you stay focused on the task at hand.

You may come up with your own unique method to let your
conscious mind be occupied and this is great. Usually you may
find yourself developing some habit down the line that helps
you when you do psychic readings. Some people discourage
using these crutches, but if they work for you and they are easy
to do, that is perfectly fine. The only caveat is to watch out that
you do not come up with an elaborate process that must be
done every time you do a reading. Make sure you choose or
allow yourself a crutch that is easily transferable from one
situation to the next.

The Internet is a Good Resource

I find that a lot of times psychics don't want to get online and
research information because they feel like it is "cheating".
They feel like they should just know everything about whatever
it is they are supposed to know about.

But…guess what…that is not always the case. Sometimes you
will receive information that you do not know how to interpret.
Remember how we talked about how sometimes you might be
wrong because you misinterpret a symbol, well, if you use a
resource like the internet to learn more about that specific
symbol then maybe you would understand it better.

In my world, there is no harm in researching information on
the internet. I do not research people or names, but the images
that come into my mind. Sometimes I learn a great deal of new
information while doing a reading because I am led to facts I
never knew about. I've had guides show me lifetimes where

they were Mongolian warriors. A quick search online will show me that the outfit they pictured themselves in is exactly what they looked like. Personally, before doing that type of reading, I was not aware of what exactly Mongolian warriors looked like, so it was nice to have that external confirmation.

But it is not just archaic knowledge. I have one guide that likes to reference movies and popular culture that I am not too aware of and sometimes have a difficult time understanding. A quick google search helps me understand what they are referring to. I have learned many songs from this guide that I was not aware of before. Lyrics to most songs are available very easily online and they tend to provide great insight into situations and people. If you are clairaudient and can pick up on lyrics, you can them search out what song they come from online.

Using the internet does not only help you learn more information it also helps with confidence. You can receive information about a topic you had no clue about, like how the ancient Greeks and Egyptians actually communicated with each other, then go online and see that this is in fact the case. Using the internet to confirm the information you receive is a great way to validate that you are actually receiving information from outside yourself.

Basically, I am reiterating here that using technology, which includes the internet, is not a bad thing for a psychic. These are resources that are available to you and you should use them. Being a psychic does not mean that you have to live without technology.

Food and Psychic Abilities

Food seems to be a sensitive topic for some individuals, but I wanted to include a little information about it because, for some people, what you eat and drink can make a difference in your ability to focus on your psychic senses.

First, let me preface this by saying that everyone is unique. Some of this information may fit your sensitivities and some may not. Pay attention to your body and how it responds, and you will find what works for you and what doesn't.

What is common for most individuals is that food tends to lower your vibrational state and thus your ability to connect with your intuition. Depending on your preferences, you may find that not eating right before a reading or having an hour or two between eating a meal and doing a reading is a good idea. Or perhaps just having something light and not a heavy meal is what is right for you.

Another thing to be cognizant of is that meat tends to have a lower vibration and has a more grounding type of energy to it so eating a lot of meat may hamper your readings. I am not saying you need to be a vegan or vegetarian, just be aware of when you consume meat and pay attention to if it effects your ability to receive clear information.

You can also use food after you do a high vibrational reading to then ground yourself. I have known psychics who wait until the end of the day and then have a steak for dinner to ground their energy and center them at the end of the day. Personally, I occasionally like to have a piece of dark chocolate when my readings are done for the day to ground my energy.

In terms of what you drink, there are some teas that are said to increase your psychic abilities and you can look into these if you choose. I have not found this to be the case, although drinking a comforting cup of tea does put me in a receptive mood just because it helps me to relax.

Caffeine in your drink may also be something to be aware of. This is another one of those items that I have not found to make a difference personally, but some people with caffeine sensitivities may find it either easier or harder to do a reading after consuming coffee or caffeinated tea. Pay attention to your body to see if it makes a difference for you.

Some psychics also refuse to drink alcoholic beverages while doing readings while others finds it helps them to relax enough to open up to their senses. Too much alcohol, however, is known to greatly reduce psychic abilities and you can find some highly sensitive individuals become dependent on alcohol when they have not been trained in how to block and shield their energy. There are also the ethics of doing readings while drinking that come into play which is something you will have to determine yourself. I do not have experience with alcohol so this is one that you will need to navigate yourself and find what is right for you.

Overall, what you see is that it is important to pay attention and recognize if the food you are eating and what you are drinking has an impact on you. It may not and that is perfectly fine. Some individuals may be super sensitive to some substances and not to others. Watch how you respond and that will tell you what is right for you.

Learning

Perhaps the one thing I think is by far the most important thing to do to help you with your psychic abilities is to spend some time learning about whatever interests you. I know, not something you really think about, but learning new information is actually something that can greatly increase your abilities as a psychic.

The thing about reading energy is that the spirit world communicates in symbols. Symbols in terms of pictures or words play a large part in your psychic dictionary. The more symbols you have available to you the more variety and depth you can offer in a reading.

What I am saying is, if you have an interest in an area, it is a great idea to learn more about that subject. For example, if you have a desire to be a medical intuitive who assists individuals in finding the areas of problem in their body, knowing the different organs, structures and bones in a body will greatly help. I am not a medical intuitive and do not have this knowledge, so when I receive information about a blockage somewhere or a medical symptom, a lot of the time I have difficulty in knowing what exactly is being conveyed. Spending time learning about the body system would greatly increase a medical intuitive's ability to communicate pertinent information.

For general psychics, I have found learning about history to be very important. There have been numerous times that I have stumbled with information I received because I was not aware of a certain part of history - which is also why I find the internet to be a wonderful tool so that I can look up this information and learn more about it.

But don't feel that your area of interest is wasted. Even learning about popular culture can help with psychic readings. I have had spirit guides present themselves in soccer uniforms to show what region or country they are relating to. And, as I have stated previously, I have found songs and lyrics to play a large part in some spirit's communication methods. You may even find that knowing a little bit about popular culture helps you read an individual better because you will know what certain symbols mean in relation to their interests.

Whatever your area of interest, I highly recommend spending time learning. Do not feel your time is being wasted or could be used better if you choose to watch a popular tv show or movie. If you feel drawn to it there may be a reason for it. Perhaps a scene will spark a past life memory, or it will be a client's favorite movie.

Learning is always happening, and it is a great way to increase your ability to give quality psychic readings. Don't look down on your interests, you may find they help you to a greater degree than you could have imagined.

Pay Attention to Other Psychics

Similar to learning, I find it very helpful to watch how other psychics and mediums work and see if you can use any of the techniques that they offer. Some advice I heard early on in my psychic journey was to read the biographies of other famous psychics and I found this very helpful. It is great to hear the process other psychics use to develop their abilities.

One thing that becomes pretty clear once you start reading and learning about other psychics is that they do not always have big experiences as children. Instead they had an interest in the psychic world and put in the time and effort to develop their abilities. Yes, some will tell stories of seeing apparitions in their bedrooms while young, but this is then usually followed by time spent honing their skill.

Learning how other psychics developed and use their abilities is a great way for you to see what potential you have as well. You can even take some of their techniques and try them out for yourself.

When you start learning about famous psychics you will also find that this ability isn't something new, but there have been psychics throughout history. You may even want to add a few of the famous spiritualists from a few hundred years ago to your list of who to check out.

I have found reading about psychics a great way to not only learn new ideas to try out, but also validate my own personal journey. Some of the biggest names out there in the psychic world spent years and years honing their craft. You shouldn't put pressure on yourself to get crystal clear answers right away if even these individuals after decades of experience don't always receive clear answers.

Along with reading biographies, it may be helpful to check out a few of the shows psychics have made throughout the years. Watching how psychic and mediums actually explain the information they are receiving can be helpful to your own process. Try out a variety of different shows and see if you are drawn to one type of reading style more than another.

Acknowledge Information

Many practicing psychics are aware of one key feature of psychic ability. The more that you acknowledge it, label it and pay attention to it, the more your psychic ability will increase. This isn't just the case with psychics, this phenomenon effects all areas of your life.

The thing about psychic insights is that you have likely been having them your whole life, just we do not currently live in a culture that teaches you what they are or that they are something to pay attention to. If our educational system was set up differently, with classes on meditation and paying attention to the mind, then you would likely realize right away that you are super psychic. But since our culture focuses on what can be seen and observed with our physical senses, those senses in the mind and energy field are easily dismissed.

Now that you know that you are having psychic insight – what should you do? Label it. Say, even just to yourself, that you know something because you are a psychic. I've done this verbally in my own life. When I "know" that my mother's lost phone is in the trunk of her car - it is because I am psychic. When I can find my husband's keys in the first place I look – because I'm psychic.

For me, labeling and acknowledging out loud these occurrences of receiving psychic insight not only helps me to grow my psychic ability, it also helps the people around me to start to notice when they have their own insights and acknowledge them as such. Just don't be too annoying about this – no one wants to hear they are psychic in the middle of a Catholic mass. Acknowledging your abilities in your mind to yourself is a good thing to do as well.

You will start to see that the more you tell yourself that you are psychic and label the times you are receiving information, the more you will actually realize that you have had these abilities all along, you just weren't recognizing them for what they really are.

Patience

One key attribute in developing your psychic abilities is the skill of patience. There are many stories around of individuals who have had a near death experience and then come back with heightened psychic abilities. But, for the majority of us, that is not an experience that is likely to happen or that we necessarily want to happen.

Instead, we must learn to develop these psychic abilities ourselves and this is something that actually takes a lot of time and patience. We currently live in a society where we like immediate gratification, we don't like to put in the work unless we can see the result right away. But as any body builder will tell you, you aren't likely to lift a ton of weight the first time you enter a gym. Similarly, you likely won't be able to see a full psychic picture or communicate with your dead grandmother in excruciating detail the first time you try. Sure, this may happen for some of you, let's not discount that, but, for most, this isn't something that is likely to happen.

Instead, you are likely going to need some patience and perseverance. Even if you don't think you have psychic abilities or if you keep getting information correct, you will find that if you are patient and stick with it, you will eventually see that you are psychic. This is a skill that sometimes takes years to develop, but it will develop if you are patient.

Patience also comes in handy when you want verification for information you receive. You won't always know right away if you are "right" or maybe even what the information you receive actually means. There are plenty of times I receive an image or symbol and have to wait for the energy to play out to understand what it means.

Patience is a big virtue in the psychic world. Don't give up on your psychic abilities, instead practice them every day and you will see the results.

Phrasing Your Questions

This is probably something you don't give much thought to but has a big impact on the information you receive. The way you phrase a question you want to receive information about will impact what information you receive.

I find this especially pertinent with individuals who ask a broad general question expecting a specific answer. When reading energy, you end up getting a response that is in line with the question you ask.

If you say you want to know about your career and ask about the energy surrounding your career, you are likely to get a broad answer. You might receive information that now is a good time to invest in strategies and skills that will help you in the future or that you can expect some growth in the next year, but you are not super likely to learn what job you will get, because that is not the question you asked.

If you want to know what type of job is best suited for you, then ask that. If you want to know if you should go for a degree in accounting or a degree in marketing, ask that. The more specific your question is, the more specific the answer you are going to get will be.

In the same regard, if you don't want to know, don't ask. I once heard a story of a woman who went to a palm reader and the palm reader said she was going to get a divorce. The woman was a Catholic and said that wasn't possible because she didn't believe in divorce. Well…guess what happen just a decade later. She and her husband filed papers for divorce.

If you are not going to be able to accept a truthful answer why ask in the first place? Rejecting the information you receive as improbable does not mean it isn't going to happen. If you don't want to know, don't ask.

Because the phrasing of questions is so important, a lot of times I like to ask a question in a variety of different ways and look at it from different angles. Usually I like to get a base reading on the "general energy" but then I will get more specific and ask detailed questions. This way I am able to create a broad landscape and then narrow down my focus.

For example, when looking at relationship questions, I usually ask for the general energy of the relationship and then take time looking at it from both individual's perspectives - how A feels about B, how B feels about A. Looking at a relationship from multiple sides is a great way to see more of the energy and understand how it is playing out from each individual's perspective.

It may also be helpful to come up with some general go-to questions you like to ask to get you started on a question or topic. This way you can anticipate the type of answers you will be receiving.

Your Belief System

Now we are going to talk about something that may not seem related to your psychic abilities and development but actually is a key to helping you advance and understand your abilities. Basically, you need to take some time and figure out what it is that you actually believe in spiritually. It is okay to not know, but you need to at least think about it.

There is a lot about the psychic world which centers around believing in what you can't see - using your intuitive senses to understand the world on a deeper level. Within this process it helps to have some context for yourself in how you fit the experiences you have.

It is okay for your beliefs to evolve as your experiences do, but it also is very helpful to have a foundation to build off of. Do you believe in spirit guides? What is your idea or thought process about God or the divine? Do you believe in angels? Do you believe in ghosts and reincarnation?

Having answers to some of these basic questions can help you frame your references and experiences. You don't have to find a religion that meets all these criteria, because it is very likely that there isn't a specific religion that encompasses all the experiences you have, but it is also okay if you do find a religion or practice a religion that speaks to you.

Many religious figures throughout history were actually very advanced psychic and intuitive individuals. Don't be afraid to research this or to form your own opinions. Your belief system will help you grow and find a way to process what you learn throughout your psychic development.

In particular, you will find a lot of psychics talking about spirit guides. This is one of my main areas of interest, so I mention them frequently. Personally, I find I have a connection with my guides which helps me to understand and process psychic information. If this isn't your belief system that is fine, but it is helpful to at least think about what your belief system is.

You will also find that there is some overlap between certain religions and spiritual practices and different psychic techniques and development processes. Many great psychics and mediums in our modern era grew up in the Catholic Church, and I do not think that is a coincidence. Many of the practices that Catholics learn from an early age actually help in the psychic development process.

There are also other religions that are based on the very premise of psychic abilities such as Spiritualism. Spiritualism has taken a backseat in today's society, but it used to be the predominant method for many mediums to learn how to communicate with the spirit world. Many famous modern-day mediums trained and learned their technique by going to Spiritualist development circles and churches.

Figuring out where you stand on some basic ideas of the universe will be very beneficial to you as you progress in your development. It is also okay and expected that some of your beliefs and ideas may shift and change as you experience new and different avenues in the unseen world.

Open your mind up to the idea of the unknown and see where your belief system leads you.

Ethics in Psychic Readings

Ethics is sometimes a boring topic, but it is actually a really important one to think about in regard to psychic readings. And thinking about it is the key word in that sentence. I recommend to every new or developing psychic to take some time to contemplate different ethical scenarios and decide for yourself, ahead of time how you will handle them.

Some of these situations are ones that may not ever happen, but, if they do you will want to have a pre-planned idea of how you will respond. With others you may want to head them off before they have the potential to occur by providing a written statement of what types of readings are acceptable and which are not. And with others, you may find that your opinions change over time as you expand your abilities and practices.

There may also be some legal implications to doing certain types of readings, so looking up the laws where you practice may be something you want to look into, especially if you end up charging money or accepting trade for readings. But, regardless of if you are doing readings for free or for money, there are some ethical considerations you will want to have in mind.

My advice is don't be afraid to change your opinions but don't let other's change them for you. The most important thing in any decision is that you keep to what you feel is right. This may be different than what other people believe and that is fine. You do you.

With that said, I am not going to tell you a strict regimen of what you should or shouldn't do, but instead give you some scenarios to think about and let you know how I navigate these different ethical situations. Then it is your turn to figure out how you would feel most comfortable in these different types of situations.

Friends and Family

Very probably the first ethical dilemma you are going to encounter is whether or not to do readings for your friends and family members. A lot of the time they are the ones that will be more than willing to be your "test subject" or to beg you for a reading when they learn that you are working on developing your psychic skills.

But, in these instances, you are going to need to decide if this is something you are comfortable doing or not. You may form your opinion on an individual case by case basis or just have a broad statement of whether or not you are comfortable doing readings for this group of people.

Some things to consider is if the individual will tease you about a reading, especially if they feel that you did not get the information correct. Is the friend or family member the type to be open minded or are they going to just shut down anything if they don't think it is true themselves? And how do you respond to this type of reaction? Are you confident in your abilities that a little verbal play won't upset you or knock you off your game, or will this end up hurting your feelings and making you doubt yourself?

Also, it is helpful to realize that some people want psychic readings because they want someone to blame when things go "wrong". They may use you as a scapegoat if they follow your psychic advice and things don't work out how they want them to work out. Be aware of the personality of the individual you are reading and if they are likely to do this to you. Remember, sometimes psychic readings are wrong for a reason, sometimes an individual needs to go through a situation to learn their earthly lessons, will the person you are reading for blame you instead of doing the spiritual work themselves?

Then there are the type of people who ask for your advice and then don't follow through with it. You may see an elaborate scenario in your mind of how their life will turn out if they follow one path or do a certain activity, then the person in question just stays where they are and doesn't make any effort. Is this going to upset you seeing your friend or family member remain stagnant in their life when you know there are greater possibilities out there for them?

So, what do I do? I do read for family and friends, but I won't do certain types of readings for certain individuals. In general, I won't do relationship readings for those in long term relationships and there are some individuals who I choose not to read. As I became more confident in my abilities I slowly opened up the individuals I was willing to read as I knew their

opinions would not affect my belief in myself, but when I was
just starting out I learned pretty early on that the teasing aspect
of family and friends did affect me. With time and confidence,
I am sure in my abilities so that isn't an issue. However, it did
take time and a lot of external validation of my abilities to get
to that place of confidence, so I am well aware that it is
something to consider when a family member or friend asks for
a reading.

Under the Influence

A common occurrence and ethical dilemma for those that do
readings at parties is whether or not they feel comfortable
doing a reading for an individual who is under the influence of
alcohol or other substances. This is also the case if you choose
to do readings in different establishments such as restaurants or
bars.

Again, like all these topics, this is a personal choice and may
depend on how under the influence the individual in question
is. This may also tailor how you do a reading. Doing a
lighthearted reading for someone who has had a few too many
glasses of wine may be a fun event but trying to get serious and
talk about major life decisions or even spirit guides may not be
the thing to do.

Something to think about before finding yourself in this
situation is what type of reading you are willing to do for an
individual under the influence or if you feel more comfortable
just not even offering to do a reading. Also consider how the
other person may or may not respond to the idea of getting a
reading and why they chose to consume substances in the first
place.

An individual may feel nervous getting a reading and thus use a substance to calm their nerves. Or they may feel like a reading is silly and they do not need to take the situation seriously. Or they could have an addiction that needs to be addressed.

Personally, I have avoided this topic for the most part by doing the majority of my readings virtually. However, I know I do not handle the vibrations of individuals under the influence well and that they would likely "throw me off" so I would not be willing to do a reading in that situation. But remember, you may be different so you need to form your own opinions here. And my personal opinion on this matter may change in the future depending on the situation.

Reading for Other People Not Present

Many times, people will ask for a psychic reading, but then they will want to know about someone else. They will want information on a potential partner or co-worker. In these situations, you need to decide if you feel it is ethical to read an individual who did not ask for a reading.

Many times, this question is unavoidable in relationship readings. You are going to have to read the other party to a relationship to see how the dynamic and energy is running. If you feel strongly about this, you may want to get the other individual's consent before doing a reading.

Personally, I will do relationship readings without the other party's consent, but I am careful how I phrase the answers and what I actually look at. I won't disclose any deep dark secret of the other individual, but I will look to see how their general energy about the individual or relationship is leaning.

This can also come into question when you are asked to do a reading as a birthday present or for a special occasion. You will find that psychic readings actually make really great and unique present ideas. Sometimes you can head these off by doing a "gift certificate" or suggestion that the birthday individual contacts you directly, but other times you will just have to decide for yourself. I do offer gift certificates if asked, but I am also willing to do a reading as a gift as long as I can send the reading directly to the individual recipient and not the gift giver. I also do not read sensitive subjects for these types of readings, but you will likely find that general readings are what people want the majority of the time.

Reading other individuals just because someone is curious is a no-go zone for me. There must be a reason for a reading to take place before I do it. I am not going to do a psychic reading to spy on your Aunt Martha, that just isn't ethical for me.

Celebrities

A side category of reading for other people is whether or not you are comfortable reading celebrities. You will find some psychics use celebrity readings as a way to garner attention and get clients interested in their readings. Other individuals will not feel comfortable reading celebrities just for fun or to satisfy the curiosity of fans.

This is a category I have many opinions about, but also involves some additional metaphysical and energy thoughts that some people do not take the time to consider. Personally, I do not do celebrity readings as I find them an invasion of the privacy of the celebrity.

Also, something that will trip up readers is that it is very easy to read the energy around a celebrity as their PR mask and not their actual energy. Celebrities that have a lot of attention surrounding them tend to also have a sort of energetic bubble that is attached to their energy and it is super easy to mistake that for their actual energy if you don't know what you are looking for (in the metaphysical world these are called egregore).

It is also helpful, if you choose to do celebrity readings, to know a little about the current trends in celebrity management. People love to do relationship readings for celebrities but there are a significant number of celebrity relationships which are strictly created for PR or distraction. This is also the case for individuals who are closeted and use relationships as a way to distract the public from their true relationships.

Before doing a celebrity reading, be aware of where you stand on the subject. Figure out whether you feel that it is okay to do this type of reading for fun and realize that there is a high chance you may not actually be reading the individual you think you are.

There is also a difference in publicizing a celebrity reading to gain attention for yourself and doing one in private to test out your psychic skills. There are still some ethical considerations to keep in mind there, but that adds another layer to consider. I will admit, I have taken a peek at a few celebrities for private confirmation of my beliefs and to test out my psychic abilities. Do what feels comfortable for you.

Death or Accident

Some individuals fear getting a psychic reading because they imagine that you are going to tell them that they are going to die or get in a horrible accident. I used to assuage individuals that I would not uncover this type of information, so they didn't need to worry…and then I started to actually receive indications of death and disease and I had to reassess my stance on this information.

I have actually found this to be an interesting ethical conundrum. If you know someone is likely to get sick and have an unfavorable outcome, do you tell them so that they can be safer, or do you not say anything and let them keep doing what they have always done? Is it okay to make people fearful or is it better to keep the information to yourself?

As with many of these ethical dilemmas this has become a case by case situation that I change and shape my opinion on as I go. For some individuals I will blatantly tell them to change a certain behavior to prevent a difficult outcome. For others I will have a trusted individual suggest some behavior changes. And for others I just keep my mouth shut.

Whether or not you pick up on this type of information, being aware of how to handle it in a sensitive and ethical manner is important. If you do see something ominous in the future for an individual, be aware of if you want to speak or not say anything at all.

Under 18

How do you feel about doing readings for individuals under 18 or children? Depending on where you live what is considered "adult" may be different, so you can use this category broadly to represent your thoughts on doing readings for those who are young.

Reading young individuals can have a large influence on them as sometimes their brains are not developed enough to understand the complexities of a situation or they do not have the emotional maturity to handle certain matters. Thinking about your opinions on this topic is important as younger individuals love readings just as much as adults.

For me this is a case-by-case, age-by-age, reading-by-reading situation. However, whatever the case, I like to have the parent's approval for a reading before I actually do one. Whether or not I will is a different matter.

First, think about the type of reading you are doing and whether or not it is appropriate for children. Certain readings are absolutely fabulous for younger individuals. What child wouldn't love to know their spirit animal? Spirit animal readings are a great way to introduce children to the world of the unseen. Other types of readings may not be appropriate depending on the age of the individual.

Speaking of ages, think about what age you feel comfortable treating more as an adult and less as a child. Do you see 15 and 16-year-olds as basically adults? This is also a line for me when I start not being willing to send parents a reading and instead insist that I will only provide the reading to the kid, especially depending on the type of reading. If the child chooses to share it with the parent is up to them, but at a certain point I feel compelled to give the child that choice and treat them as an adult to a degree.

So, take some time to think about what type of readings you feel comfortable doing for children or whether you would prefer just to have a strict age policy. Also decide if there are any stipulations that go along with this type of reading such as parental consent or who is present during a reading. And remember, your ideas and opinions may change but it is good to have a general idea before you get put into a situation you aren't comfortable with.

Legal, Medical and Professional Readings

I would advise some caution with deciding to provide any sort of legal, medical or professional advice or information during a psychic reading. This is one of those areas where you may want to pay attention to your local laws and perhaps even provide a disclaimer if you are doing any professional readings.

In addition to any actual laws to be aware of, there are some ethical considerations to take into account. How sure are you of the medical or legal information you are providing? What if someone uses your advice in a way that was harmful to yourself or others?

Even though I have a background as a lawyer, I do not like to give legal advice in any capacity. I also don't find too many people coming to psychics for actual legal advice, but it can and does happen. I recommend talking in terms of general energy and straying away from any hard and fast legal information.

It is much more common to run into the medical advice conundrum. Medical intuitives and psychics are becoming much more common along with energy healers. Knowing where you stand on this subject before it comes up in a reading can be important. When reading individual's energy, it is easy to run into health problems as their energy signature is sometimes very distinct and common to read.

Personally, for medical readings I always like to give a caveat to seek professional medical advice on any questions they may have. This takes me a step away from any reading and basically says "hey don't blame the psychic for this one". I also do not have a background in the physical body, nor do I know too much about it so my readings in this vein will not be as detailed as someone who focuses on that area.

In general, I recommend caution on any matters where people are using your psychic insights to make any major decisions. Sometimes what they want is a scapegoat and it is better to not let you be that individual.

Receiving Unsolicited Information

As you start to open up and train your psychic abilities, you may find yourself receiving information and impressions as you go about your day to day reality. The question then becomes - what do you do with this information you receive? Do you tell the individual what you picked up or do you keep the information to yourself?

With the popularity of certain shows showing mediums going up to random strangers on the street telling them that their long dead great aunt has a message for them, it seems like the ethics around this matter have become clouded. But you should know, that there are other ways to handle situations like this and what is ethical is a matter of your own standards and the situation at hand.

You may find that sometimes you are receiving information about another person for you yourself, sort of a confirmation of your abilities and not something that needs to be passed along. I remember distinctly a time sitting around watching my daughter's dance class where one of the other dance mom's auras suddenly became very visible. In this situation I did not stop the conversation to then talk about what was going on in their aura. Instead, I kept that information to myself and did not let on what I was receiving. This was what was best for me personally and ethically in that situation and thus I followed it.

Sometimes you may find yourself in a situation where you pick up on a message from a deceased relative or something that seems very pertinent. In these situations, it is best to look to your own personal ethics on what to do. And, if you are ever unsure, I always recommend asking your guides or your intuition what to do. This may provide the answer you need.

What I personally do not find ethical, and what truly happens in a lot of those popular tv shows, is when you actively try to read complete strangers to receive information. If you really watch those medium reality shows you will see that the medium is actively tuning in, trying to receive information, instead of randomly picking up on facts.

A true psychic knows how to put up a shield or block out information when they are not doing a reading. Closing down your psychic senses is an important task and something that should be accomplished. Yes, occasionally information will seep through, but if you are receiving detailed messages from beyond the grave regularly when going about your day to day reality you need to work on shutting down and protecting your energy field.

Think about what you would do in this type of situation, when you pick up information while going about your normal daily reality. In most cases you will see that this ethical dilemma is very situation dependent and each instance may be different. Yes, sometimes it is appropriate to pass on a message while other times it is best to keep it to yourself. If you are ever in doubt of what to do ask for guidance and then listen to what your intuition tells you.

Conclusion

Developing your psychic abilities is a wonderful and rewarding activity. We are all born with some psychic intuition and it is up to us on whether or not we decide to develop it. This is something that comes naturally to some individuals and for others it may take time to develop and really hone the craft, but it is possible for everyone.

Give yourself the time and practice to develop your abilities. This can be a fun process as you learn what psychic abilities actually are and start to understand that you have likely been using them your entire life. A little work every day will help you to develop and expand these natural abilities.

What I always say is that the most important thing in any activity is that you are having fun. If it starts to become more burdensome or frustrating, take a break. You can always come back to it at a later time. Let yourself enjoy the process and make it your own.

About the Author

Mary Shannon is an intuitive consultant, an author, and a mystic. Through her website, sevencupsmystic.com, you can order professional readings, find links to all her books, and check out her weekly blog posts. Mary has clients throughout the world and sees it as her mission to help individuals learn to connect to their own intuition.